PRAISE FOR

Eco-yards

Eco-yards proposes a partnership approach with the garden and inspires homeowners to build peaceful, practical yards. Rama is a hands-on gardener who explains — in great detail— everything from building soil to creating sustainable landscapes. Read about it here and then get out and practice what Rama preaches.

> — DONNA BALZER, BScA, horticulturist and co-host of the internationally broadcast television show *Bugs & Blooms*

Let's face it. It won't be long before everyone will simply have to have a sustainable yard. Either your neighbors will push you into it, a government will make you or you won't be able to buy dangerous 'icides and harmful, chemical fertilizers because they will finally be banned. So why wait to have a safe, environmentally friendly, yard? Use the simple instructions laid out in *Eco-yards* by Laureen Rama and have one now. Written by an experienced landscaper designer (who clearly understands a thing or two about the soil food web and my friends the microbes), *Eco-yards* translates all the completed design "stuff" into terms you can understand and act upon, and then shows you how to make your yard beautiful, the earth-friendly way. Don't wait until you are forced to have a sustainable yard, start now with *Eco-yards*. Its a reference now, for the future!

> —JEFF LOWNEFELS, co-author, *Teaming with Microbes: A Gardener's Guide to the Soil Food Web*

Laureen Rama has produced a valuable resource for the urban homeowner that focuses on ecology and presents healthy soil as a foundation for a healthy and functioning yard.

> —KEN FRY. Ph.D., co-author *Garden Bugs of Alberta: Gardening to Attract, Repel and Control*

Are you among the increasing number of homeowners seeking alternatives to conventional lawncare practices? Here is your answer! *Eco-yards* is a gentle, practical and inspiring guide to help you transform your yard into a diverse, healthy and sustainable landscape.

—MYRNA PEARMAN, co-author, *NatureScape Alberta: Creating and caring for wildlife habitat at home*

A rich compost of the practical and the scientific... this is a book for every gardener concerned for the health of the environment.

—ROBERTA REES, author, *Long after Fathers*

Eco-yards

Simple steps to earth-friendly landscapes

LAUREEN RAMA

with contributions by Caron Wenzel

NEW SOCIETY PUBLISHERS

Printed in Canada. First printing January 2011.

New Society Publishers acknowledges the support of the Government of Canada through the
Book Publishing Industry Development Program (BPIDP) for our publishing activities.

Paperback ISBN: 978-0-86571-682-7
eISBN: 978-1-55092-466-4

To order directly from the publishers, please call toll-free (North America) 1-800-567-6772,
or order online at www.newsociety.com

Any other inquiries can be directed by mail to:

New Society Publishers
P.O. Box 189, Gabriola Island, BC V0R 1X0, Canada
(250) 247-9737

New Society Publishers' mission is to publish books that contribute in fundamental ways to building
an ecologically sustainable and just society, and to do so with the least possible impact on the
environment, in a manner that models this vision. We are committed to doing this not just through
education, but through action. Our printed, bound books are printed on Forest Stewardship Council-
certified acid-free paper that is 100% post-consumer recycled (100% old growth forest-free),
processed chlorine free, and printed with vegetable-based, low-VOC inks, with covers produced
using FSC-certified stock. New Society also works to reduce its carbon footprint, and purchases
carbon offsets based on an annual audit to ensure a carbon neutral footprint. For further information,
or to browse our full list of books and purchase securely, visit our website at: www.newsociety.com

NEW SOCIETY PUBLISHERS
www.newsociety.com

Mixed Sources
Product group from well-managed
forests and other controlled sources
www.fsc.org Cert no. SW-COC-1271
© 1996 Forest Stewardship Council

Library and Archives Canada Cataloguing in Publication

Rama, Laureen
    Eco-yards : simple steps to earth-friendly landscapes / Laureen Rama ; with contributions by
Caron Wenzel.

Includes index.
ISBN 978-0-86571-682-7

    1. Organic gardening. 2. Garden ecology. 3. Gardening--Environmental
aspects. I. Wenzel, Caron, 1954- II. Title.

SB453.5.R34 2010   635'.0484   C2010-906559-X

To my father, Bill Rama,
a chemical engineer
who came to support
the concept of eco-yards,
and who always
supported me

Contents

Preface

I wrote this book for all those who want their yards—the small or large plots of land they steward—to be part of the solution to today's environmental challenges.

It can bring despair to know the crisis our ecosystem is in right now. I have found that hope comes through taking action. My desire is that *Eco-yards* brings you encouragement to take action and find hope in working with your own yard.

There are many books that explain the state of environmental crisis we are in and the challenges we face. This book is largely about solutions—actions from small to large—that you can take in your yard. I want to show you that in simple steps you can turn your yard into an eco-friendly sanctuary. In so doing you help restore the local and global ecosystem.

This book is also a call to beauty. We could have urban landscapes that are so much more beautiful and nurturing to our souls—wild, varied, full of songbirds, color and movement throughout the year.

So let's do it!

Laureen Rama

Special note to apartment and condo dwellers: Yes, you have a yard too! Whether it's your balcony, a window box or the grounds of your building, you can probably garden your little patch of soil in a more eco-friendly way. You can also work with the owner or management or the condo board of directors to have your grounds maintained differently or re-landscaped. In the long run this usually saves money on maintenance—a good incentive. Show them this book!

Introduction

VISIONING OUR CITIES AND TOWNS AS LUSH GARDENS

In 2007, as I was flying home over the prairies to the city of Calgary, I looked out over the fields below and reflected on what I knew about the many chemicals farmers are using. Some part of me felt the sterility, the barrenness of the endless grainfields below. As we neared Calgary, I felt despair at knowing how the city too had been sterilized. I imagined driving home along boulevards of dusty, dry, shaved grass reeking of acrid pesticides, with my heart racing and mind reeling from reaction to the pesticides (I experienced chemical sensitivities at that time). I realized I was hating my city. I wanted to fight against those who advocated for pesticide use. I was in a reactive, battle-ready frame of mind—a state you could describe as warrior-like.

These thoughts and emotions were definitely unpleasant and not working for me! My stomach was in a knot, I had a headache and felt crabby. I wondered what this vision and energy were creating in the world when they were doing all this to me!

I decided that, from then on, it would be more healthy to focus on my positive vision for Calgary landscapes and my love for Calgary — the reasons I live and do this work here. As the plane banked, I could see the downtown cluster of buildings, the two blue-green rivers that flow through the city, the prairie on the outskirts of the city and the foothills and mountains beyond. I imagined Calgary as a place where the boulevards and open spaces were

3

> ## Let Your Politicians See Your Vision!
>
> If you share this vision of a healthy, green city or town with naturalized green space and cosmetic pesticide use phased out, contact your municipal, provincial or state and federal politicians. Politicians usually want to hear from their constituents and they are the ones who have the power to put your vision into action.

naturalized—planted with bushes, trees and perennials that would offer a feast of flowering and color throughout the year; yards were varied and interesting; meadowlarks and warblers trilled; the smells were of healthy soil and flowers; community vegetable, herb and flower gardens were in every neighborhood; butterflies floated and bees buzzed.

Invigorated and more relaxed after this vision, I felt the importance of continuing to positively envision beautiful city landscapes and of sensing the beauty in the landscapes as they are now. I remembered that soil micro-organisms are amazingly hardy and resilient and can come back after chemical treatment—the land will recover to vitality and fruitfulness.

I felt hopeful. I remembered that one of the most effective ways to create change is to hold a hopeful and inspiring vision that motivates you and can motivate others.

SUGGESTIONS FOR READING THIS BOOK

This book is meant to provide both inspiration for and information on gardening in an eco-friendly way. I suggest reading Chapters 1 to 3, Chapter 8 and Overview for a solid grounding in eco-yards. These, plus parts of Chapters 6 and 11, aim at giving you some background and motivation. The rest of the book will, I hope, provide you with the practical information you need to turn inspiration to practice. Read these other chapters as you need them to take action. Some of the information is repeated as it's assumed you will dip in and out of the book.

Throughout the book are drawings of soil micro-organisms, the key to healthy soil and the foundation of a healthy eco-yard.

I feel if these vital beings, invisible to the naked eye, become more real to you, you will landscape in ways that nurture them.

Chapters 1 to 3 provide the how, the what and the why of eco-yards. Read these if you want to understand the rationale behind eco-gardening. Knowing why you are taking the steps to create an eco-yard can keep you motivated! Chapter 1, The Gardener, is about how you can reframe your thinking to approach landscaping with an attitude conducive to Earth-friendly action. Chapter 2, What Is an Eco-yard?, lays out general principles of eco-friendly landscaping; it's an ecology primer. Chapter 3, Why Eco-yards?, explains why Earth-friendly landscaping is necessary for the environment and human health.

Chapters 4 and 5 are about maintaining your yard in an eco-friendly way. Chapter 4, Eco-maintenance, addresses general maintenance. Chapter 5, Weeds and Bugs, shares some strategies to work with these lively challenges!

Lawn is typically the highest-maintenance, least Earth-friendly landscape, and much of this book is devoted to the hows and whys of replacing lawn with a more natural landscape. Chapter 6, What's in a Lawn?, provides a history of how lawn came to be the dominant feature of our urban yards. As a step to replacing your lawn, and because lawn sometimes is appropriate, the chapter includes a section on ways to transition your lawn to more Earth-friendly grasses for the locale and how to keep your lawn lush and healthy.

Chapter 7, Making Beds to Replace Your Lawn, spells out ways to replace your lawn—some may be easier than you think! Mulch—organic cover to keep your beds moist and weed-free—is covered in detail.

Chapter 8, Soil: A Feeding Frenzy, unlocks the amazing world of soil micro-organisms and how they interact with plants to feed each other and the world!

Chapter 9, The Wonders of Compost, details how to make compost, worm compost and actively aerated compost tea, so you can build healthy soil in your yard.

Chapters 10 and 11 suggest points to ponder in designing an eco-yard. Chapter 10, Designing Your Eco-yard, includes general guidelines for the design process, tips on hiring a designer/landscaper, Earth-friendly design principles, feng shui design principles, guidelines on choosing plants, and designing like a musical composer! Chapter 11, Water-wise Design, shows you how to design a yard you'll need to water very little, if at all.

Chapter 12, Growing Vegetables, highlights ways to grow food in your yard and, in particular, features Caron Wenzel's eco-yard near Chicago. Wenzel is a contributor to the book, having written the base of the making compost and worm composting sections of Chapter 9 and also this chapter on growing vegetables.

Finally, the Overview is a summary of how to garden the eco-yards way. If you only read one chapter, read this one. Notes after each chapter detail references for information in that chapter. The Resources section, near the end of the book, points you to where you can find more information or the supplies needed to create your eco-yard.

I invite you to enjoy thinking about, designing, creating and nurturing your eco-yard!

1

The Gardener
(Make love not war in your eco-yard)

---

*Life is a mystery to be lived,
not a problem to be solved. —Unknown*

Amoebas

THE BIRTH OF A NEW VIEW:
THE ECO-YARDS CONCEPT

**Last year, I was asked to give a talk on chemical-free
gardening. When the coordinator sent me drafts of the
newsletter and poster blurb for the talk —Come learn
natural methods for getting rid of pests! —I realized she
and I saw gardening from very different perspectives.
I was horrified by the prospect of being boxed into a
future career of talking about vinegars and insecticidal
soap, neglecting the bigger story of how we can steward
our yards in a more ecologically friendly way.
I remembered the discomfort, during other such
talks, of answering questions mostly about how
to kill things. Once, I'd blurted at a participant,
"My forté is not killing things; I got into this line
of work because I love to plant and grow things!"**

Bless the talk coordinator, because in my struggle to explain this feeling
to her it became even clearer to me that eco-yards gardening is not
simply about replacing chemical weapons with organic weapons in a war
against pests. Eco-yards gardening is about replacing the common view
of gardening as a war to control our little plots of land with a different
view—that of gardening as a way to work in harmony with other beings
in nature to revitalize the land we steward so it is shining with health.

Growing ourselves:
Archetypes and our new role in the gardening drama

For many of us, this approach is a fundamental shift in how we view landscaping and gardening. What's the most effective way to make such a wholesale change? Embody the archetype of the Gardener rather than the Warrior.

The concept of archetypes was developed by Carl Jung, the great Viennese psychoanalyst. He found that similar characters showed up again and again in his clients' dreams. Archetypes are the great roles we all play in our lives. They are portrayed in myth, in movies, on television, in books and in our dreams. Many writers have used various archetypes as models to work with to further personal growth and development.

Examples of Archetypes

ARCHETYPE	EXAMPLES
the Magician	Gandalf in "Lord of the Rings", Martin Luther King Jr.: "I have a dream"
the Ruler	any king or queen, Barack Obama
the Innocent	Dorothy near the beginning of "The Wizard of Oz"
the Warrior	a martial artist, a soldier
the Caregiver	Mother Teresa
the Lover	Don Juan
the Sage	Yoda in "Star Wars"
the Fool	Robin Williams in his comedy roles

Eco-yards and the Warrior

The dominant archetype in Western culture for centuries has been the Warrior—so prevalent, in fact, we often don't even notice its influence. Today, the everyday language of mainstream media is full of metaphors of war and battle, metaphors that shape the common approach to many activities. We constantly hear about "battling cancer," "the War on Terror," "the War on Drugs," "the target market," "our aim and objective," "my opponent," "our weapons."

Landscaping, too, is often thought of as a battle against plant diseases, a fight against the weather, a war on weeds, or an assault on insects to protect our lawn and trees. Is it possible to win these battles? In my experience, rarely. In real warfare, "winning" may take such massive firepower that everything is devastated; buildings are levelled, vegetation is killed, and the result is a lifeless wasteland. The civilians that warriors were trying to protect are dead or left without food, shelter or viable land.

How Do You Define "Pest"?

The Oxford Dictionary defines "pest" as "any thing or person that is noxious, destructive or troublesome; a bane, curse, plague." – *The Oxford Universal Dictionary on Historical Principles*, 3rd ed. (Oxford, Clarendon Press, 1955). By this definition, humans may be the worst pests on Earth.

The "civilians" in the urban landscaping warfare of the last 50 years are the tiny bacteria, fungi and other micro-organisms in the soil and on plant leaves that ensure plants receive the nutrients they need to grow. Soil micro-organisms are critical to life on Earth; without them plants won't grow. And all living things on Earth depend on plants. The firepower that has devastated the soil micro-organisms has usually been in the form of chemicals. This devastation may be difficult to detect because, while chemical pesticides have been used to do battle with "pests," chemical fertilizers have been used to feed the plants nutrients they can no longer readily get from the soil. So most of the plants live, but they're not as healthy and lush as they could be.

This warlike approach has been destroying the health of our soil—the basis of its fertility. We also may not notice, because it has happened over time, that in many locations there are fewer birds and insects and certainly fewer varieties, especially of some of the more delicate and beautiful species, such as songbirds. This is because of chemical use and loss of natural habitat.

The Warrior archetype is not suited to eco-yards gardening. A different set of qualities is required. Eco-yards gardening is life-affirming; it's not about win-lose. Eco-yards gardening is about partnership and cooperation with the plants, the soil and the conditions, rather than about control.

Eco-yards gardening is about supporting the ecosystem in its complexity of interactions. This does not mean there is no destruction. Creation and destruction are an essential part of the circle of life. In an eco-yard, destruction supports the ecosystem. Weeding, pruning and digging to plant are all destructive acts that support a healthy eco-yard. And in an eco-yard, whatever is destroyed usually goes into the compost pile to become new soil and food for plants.

Eco-yards gardening is about letting go of looking for silver bullets or quick fixes and having the patience to allow everything the time it needs to develop and grow and shift and die. It's not about trading in chemical weapons for potent organic ones, but rather building the health of the whole ecosystem of the yard. It's about tending and planning for the long term and being open to surprise at what unfolds.

ECO-YARDS AS NATUROPATHY

Some people compare the difference between Warrior and eco-yards gardening to the difference between conventional Western medicine and naturopathic or preventive medicine for human health. The former often relies on drugs to cure symptoms. The drugs then may cause side effects and other problems. For example, antibiotics can weaken the basic digestive system by killing off some of the beneficial bacteria that help us absorb nutrients and stay healthy. Naturopathic medicine, on the other hand, focuses on balancing and strengthening our whole body; this may, for example, involve taking probiotics (beneficial bacteria) to restore the digestive system. In preventive medicine, the focus is on taking the body to optimum health so it can naturally address any germs or diseases and stay healthy.

Taking a similar naturopathic approach to your yard really works. Why? First, because healthy plants are less susceptible to infestation by insects and disease. So-called pests—insects that eat plants, and diseases that infest plants—sense differently than humans; unhealthy plants give off a different light frequency than healthy plants, for example. To the "pests," unhealthy plants are more attractive: they're weaker, less protected by a layer of healthy microbes and therefore easier to chew through and lodge on. Who wouldn't go for the easy meal? Animal predators do the same, minimizing energy output in the hunt by picking off the weakest members of a herd (the young, the old, the sick). This process actually helps to keep the ecosystem healthy and balanced. So "pests" have their role.

Taking the naturopathic approach further, we can understand weeds as an indication that the soil minerals and chemistry are not balanced. Once the soil is more balanced, healthy plants will grow where only weeds would grow before (see Chapter 5, Weeds and Bugs).

The War on Weeds

The War on Weeds? We gave that up long ago! And everything out here at our nursery looks just fine. We hoe weeds when they're small. We mulch with wood chips to prevent weeds. And when the thistles get tall in the few areas they grow, we mow them. When lots of aphids show up on certain trees, we leave them. It's usually just a cycle: this is their year, and they'll be gone next year.

– Ken Wright, Bow Point Nursery, Springbank, Alberta

CHANGING ARCHETYPES

The Warrior archetype is so engrained in our culture that it can be difficult to think differently about landscaping and gardening. If we don't, though, we won't know how to act differently. To change our approach, we must adopt a new archetype, stepping into a different way of thinking about how to be in the world (or at least in our gardens).

Although we may not think of it as such, we step into different archetypal roles all the time. For example, a good parent will embody several archetypes at various times—the Ruler: "Everyone get ready—we're leaving in five minutes!"; the Magician: "I'll kiss that hurt spot and it will get better"; and the Caregiver: "Let me give you a hug and a bath and then put you to bed." A parent may shift archetypes from moment to moment, sometimes embodying several at once.

Embodying the appropriate archetype is important to play a role fully or to make the most of a situation. For example, you probably won't have any fun at a party until you activate at least a bit of the Fool archetype within you. If you are engaged in a martial art, you want to embody the Warrior archetype to avoid getting hurt and be a worthy opponent. Acting from an inappropriate archetype can mean a lack of synchrony between thought and action. So making the switch from Warrior to Gardener is key to success in eco-gardening.

The Warrior and the Gardener

Two young men have worked with me in landscaping over the last few years. One embodies the Warrior archetype thoroughly, and I learned to have him mainly do tasks for which Warrior qualities are helpful—digging out sod, hauling soil, building walls. He has broken numerous handles of weeding tools as he tries to muscle the weeds out of the ground rather than sensing resistance and backing off from tree roots and then rocking gently to pull the weeds out. The other young man is a true Gardener. When I first saw him carry plants as if they were newborn babies, I taught him how to plant, and this is largely his task now. One of my favorite memories is coming upon him sitting in lanky lotus position, gently digging with a trowel between the rocks of a pathway as he planted low groundcovers. His rhythm was smooth, and he looked relaxed and serene, like a part of the landscape.

THE SECRET GARDEN

The best model I know of the Gardener archetype is the character Dickon in Frances Hodgson Burnett's novel *The Secret Garden* (1911).[1] The book has been made into a few movies, at least one of which should be available at your local video store or library—and may

A Gardener

already be on your children's video shelf. In the story, the 12-year-old "common cottage boy" Dickon guides a young crippled boy and his girl cousin through caring for a garden in such a way that they (along with the young boy's father) are restored to their true loving, laughing, lively and healthy selves from an earlier state of lonely unhappiness.

The story is set on the Yorkshire moors in England. Dickon spends much time out on the moors and in the garden of the estate where the two little cousins, Mary and Colin, live. Mary and Colin believe Dickon to be doing magic because he has tamed squirrels and a crow, and birds follow him and listen to him play his flute. Dickon explains that, far from magic, his close relationship with nature is a result of living on the moor so much and knowing the ways of the animals. Moreover, he "feels sometimes as if he was a bird or a rabbit himself."

Dickon has a way with plants too. He tends a vegetable and herb garden for his mother. "We'd never get on as comfortable as we do," says his mother, "if it wasn't for Dickon's garden. Anything'll grow for him. His 'taters and cabbages is twice th' size of any one else's an' they've got a flavour with 'em as nobody's has." Dickon has also planted beautiful flowers in this garden.

When the crippled little boy starts to walk, he asks Dickon if he's making the magic that helps him walk. Dickon responds, "'Tha's doing Magic thysel' .... It's same Magic as made these 'ere work out o' th' Earth ...'" Dickon then touches "with his thick boot a clump of crocuses in the grass .... 'Aye ... there couldna' be bigger Magic than that here—there couldna' be.'"

Dickon demonstrates a strong Gardener quality, continually sharing his vision of what the garden will become. He inspires the children to love tending and maintaining the garden and keeps them open to its wonder—they can't wait to get up and see what will unfold there each day.

Dickon embodies an awareness of and reverence for natural patterns, a sensitivity to all other beings, the ability to envision what could be in the garden, the know-how to create that vision (which comes from years of observing natural patterns) and the nurturing to care for all the elements of the garden. He also loves and appreciates the natural ecosystem, its complexity and surprises, and approaches it with wonder and delight. As a result, everything flourishes around Dickon: the plants, the birds and other animals in the garden—and the two children.

A real life Gardener in Oregon

As I was thinking about who, of those I knew, embodied the Gardener archetype, I had a magical experience of synchronicity—I met a Gardener. A friend took a group, including me, to lunch at a farm using organic methods near Portland, Oregon, that included a restaurant, hotel, vineyard and large gardens that provide produce to the kitchen. A woman was tending the herb garden near the restaurant, raking leaves off low strawberry plants. Someone asked, "Are you making the strawberries happy?" The woman, Leah, responded, "Yes, all it takes is a little love." I perked up, excited to meet someone who embodied the Gardener archetype. I asked her if the farm and orchard were organic, and yes, they were. I asked what she thought of my view that people often just trade in their chemical weapons for organic ones, still essentially fighting with nature. She responded

From Warrior to Gardener

Changing archetypes from Warrior to Gardener is a matter of shifting from seeing ourselves as dominant and in control of the land to understanding our role as its temporary steward, working in cooperation with its many natural processes.

A Gardener

that the people who tended the farm only used a bit of pyrethrin, considered a natural pesticide, in the greenhouse when they needed to control some insects in that unnatural environment. They used compost, compost tea and some mineral sprays in the orchard. "We weed and tend plants by hand, and once in a while I may squish some bugs. Otherwise, it all works itself out if you leave it alone." She then was silent for a minute and offered, "The most magic happens in the vegetable garden. I figure plants have egos and want to show us what they can do, so I ask them 'Who's going to show me their stuff first?' and they respond—they all seem to grow better!"

BEING A GARDENER

While the character Dickon represents the Gardener ideal, most of us probably aren't able to spend enough waking hours out of doors and in the garden to have the squirrels following us and robins talking to us! Still, we can emulate the qualities of love, connection and vision that Dickon brings to gardening.

My Gramma Belle was a Gardener in her unique way. She simply believed that anything would grow for her regardless of the conditions—and it did! She grew houseplants in what seemed like clay and baked them in her bay window, and they looked healthy and bloomed profusely. Her vegetable gardens and flowerbeds were full.

My Gramma Bertha communed every morning with her beloved Hansa rose (almost taller than she was), drinking her coffee from a teacup as, in her housecoat, she deadheaded the spent blossoms to encourage the rose to keep blooming. Her grandchildren and her sister's grandchildren came to identify the Hansa rose with her, and most of us have one in our yards—some from the original bush.

It's not surprising that "Magic" (of nature, of the moors, of healing) is a prominent theme in *The Secret Garden*. In addition to more obvious caring qualities, a true Gardener embodies and taps into what can be seen as magical qualities. When we understand that our small actions in the yard have an effect on the world at large, when we conjure a vision of our future garden, when we transform initial disappointment at rain into joy (the plants will be watered and we can take a walk in the rain or stay inside and do something else we wanted to do), we are doing Gardener magic.

While some may sense or see the actual energies of the trees and plants, simply feeling appreciation is also a sign of a Gardener. I do a small ritual of walking around my yard almost every day and saying hello in my mind to the plants and sometimes the other features in the yard (like the compost bin). Sometimes I will feel my joy at their beauty (even in the dusty early spring) as I greet them. Whether the plants feel this or not, it helps me to feel connected to them and to enjoy caring for them. I also like to imagine the microbes on the plants and in the soil and greet them too, simply to remind me they are there carrying out vital functions.

Rituals of any kind align one's body with mind and spirit and are a powerful way to strengthen commitment. Any ritual you invent that

Plants Have Feelings Too!

Research has shown that plants respond to our feelings and may have their own feelings too. Peter Tompkins and Christopher Bird used polygraph techniques (also used for lie detection!) and found that plants respond much as humans do to different situations.[2]

Recreating Eden

"Recreating Eden", a production by Canada's Vision Television, highlights a gardener and their garden on every show. The first seasons of the show are available on DVD. I've found it truly inspiring to see how gardeners around the world have had a vision and co-created with nature to build beautiful gardens.

is meaningful to you, for instance, when you break ground or plant, can help you remember and commit to the principles of eco-yards gardening.

Other ways you can reinforce the Gardener in yourself include hanging out with people who embody the Gardener archetype, reading books like *The Secret Garden* and watching movies or TV shows on gardening. Having a uniform for your Gardener archetype—a set of pants or vest, a gardening apron or gloves—can help you step into the archetype. Taking the posture of the Gardener—rounded and soft, looking or reaching up or down, aware of Earth and sky energy—may also help.

GARDENER FOR A SUSTAINABLE PLANET

This book is about how to be an eco-friendly gardener in your yard. If we are to truly develop sustainable human living on this planet, the Gardener archetype must become a norm. It is this fundamental shift in attitude and worldview about the natural world, and our place in it, that will support us in creating new ways to live and in taking action.

The Gardener is nothing new; rather, it is ancient. Most indigenous cultures approach the world this way. Our ancestors did. We have it in us. We just need to remember.

SUMMARY

- Gardening the eco-yards way requires working with nature rather than battling to control nature.

Rethinking Cottonwood Fluff

Many people blame the fluff that appears from cottonwood poplars each year for their allergies. The fluff isn't at fault—fluff is the female seed holder. The male pollen from trees and grasses is what triggers allergies. I've encouraged people to think of the fluff as magical feminine energy floating around full of seeds, just waiting to find a place to land and plant those seeds.

- Embodying the Gardener archetype rather than the Warrior archetype is the most effective way to think and act in harmony with nature.
- The Gardener archetype is needed for humans globally to restore harmony with nature.

NOTES

1. Frances Hodgson Burnett, *The Secret Garden* (New York: Dell, Yearling edition, 1987). Originally published in 1911.

2. Peter Tompkins and Christopher Bird, *The Secret Life of Plants* (New York: Harper & Row, 1973).

What Is an Eco-yard?

Not only is another world possible, she is on her way. On a quiet day, I can hear her breathing. —Arundhati Roy

Bacteria

So, what exactly is an eco-yard? An eco-yard is a landscape—usually the grounds around a home or building—with a full, rich ecosystem that is healthy and alive. At the very least, an eco-yard causes no harm in its presence or by its care, to the environment. At best, an eco-yard enhances and restores the natural environment.

The eco-yard concept embraces right relationship with the Earth—the whole Earth and all its beings—at the most local level, our own yard. An eco-yard is also an ideal to move toward, holding right relationship as an aspiration and a vision. An eco-yard is about stewardship and partnership with the natural ecosystem rather than control. Scientists are still learning about the complex interactions in nature (of which humans are a part) that support life. It seems that, whenever we do things in our landscapes much differently than does the natural world, we create a lot of unnecessary work for ourselves and hamper the natural ecosystem, not just in our yards but globally.

A diverse and healthy landscape will require less maintenance than what has been standard in the North American yard—until now. An eco-yard can look after itself with a little help from its stewards—and as much love and care as the stewards wish to lavish on their eco-yard!

GENERAL PRINCIPLES OF ECO-YARDS

Eco-yards embody five general attributes or principles. They foster and display

• a full, rich ecosystem
• diversity
• co-creation with nature
• a variety of designs
• sustainability

FULL, RICH ECOSYSTEM

An ecosystem is a system in which many species support each other in living well in a certain terrain, climate and area. So a yard can have its own ecosystem that is part of the neighborhood ecosystem, which is part of the ecosystem of a town or city, which is part of the ecosystem of the geographical region, which is part of the global ecosystem of the Earth including all of the plants, animals, birds, reptiles, rocks, rivers, mountains, oceans, fish, microbes, insects and the atmosphere.

In any ecosystem, the various plants, insects, birds, animals and other living beings come to fill niches—certain roles they play to support the other beings in the ecosystem and in which they in turn are supported. In its own niche, a plant will thrive.

Certain insects, birds and even bats can play the role of pollinator for specific plants. Plants in flower are like flashing neon lights to a pollinator and let the pollinator know that the diner is open. For example, a blueberry plant is supported in reproducing by the native bees that bring pollen to it from other blueberry plants. These bees eat nectar provided by the blueberry. Pollination by the bees allows the flower to produce berries full of seeds that will grow new blueberries. Then birds and other animals eat the blueberries. They help the blueberry plant spread to new areas by carrying seeds to other places.

Humans are part of the ecosystem too. The plants provide us with food (such as blueberries), and we can play many roles in support of plants, such as planting seeds, watering the plants, weeding, feeding the plants with compost and pruning.

Those Clever Grasses

Michael Pollan is a wonderful thinker about plants and how we interact with them as part of our ecosystem. He has written a number of books, including *The Botany of Desire*, *The Omnivore's Dilemma* and *In Defense of Food*. He has a fun take on how grasses have enticed humans into protecting their niche in the ecosystem—especially cereal grasses like rice, wheat and corn: we humans cut down trees, keep the ground clear and plant and tend the cereal grasses. If it weren't for humans, much of the global ecosystem now planted in cereal grasses would be some kind of forest or jungle.

Micro-organisms are vital to a full, rich ecosystem

While such interactions between members of an ecosystem are going on before our eyes, other vital but less visible interactions are going on among billions of micro-organisms and other members of the ecosystem, including plants. These we can only see by looking at a leaf, root or soil sample under a microscope. This teeming soup of micro-organisms (or microbes) on leaf and needle surfaces and clustered around roots is the foundation of life on Earth and life in your eco-yard. See Chapter 8, Soil: A Feeding Frenzy.

Plants release foods to the micro-organisms on their leaves and at their roots, and the micro-organisms make soil nutrients available to the plants. Without microbes, plants couldn't use the nutrients in the soil. Microbes are essential to plant life. Because everything on Earth relies directly or indirectly on plants for food at some point in the food chain, microbes are fundamental to life on Earth.

Soil micro-organisms: ciliate-eating bacteria, amoeba, nematode-eating bacteria

Aim for balance

The healthiest ecosystems contain a great diversity of species in many different niches, and all the niches are filled. In a healthy ecosystem, the various members of the ecosystem keep each other's influence and numbers in balance.

Balance is important and therefore something to consider in an eco-yard and for the ecosystem as a whole. For example, be mindful of the balance between predator and prey. Often, due to human influence, a natural predator species may be eliminated or reduced, and then another member of the ecosystem overpopulates and may ravage the species that it eats. For example, in the Chicago area, there are no natural predators for deer. So in some of the green belts, many plants that would normally grow under the trees can't because the deer eat them. Parks authorities are fencing off some areas to protect the plants.

Invasive ox-eye daisies

istockphoto.com/fotoVoyager

Also be aware of the effect on balance when a species is brought in from another ecosystem. Because the original ecosystem has no controls for that new species, it can invade and take over niches that native plants and animals had previously filled. Examples of invasive plants are Himalayan blackberries on the northwest coast of North America, ox-eye daisies in Waterton Lakes National Park in Canada and purple loosestrife in eastern North America. In your eco-yard, it is important to check with local nurseries or garden centers that the species you are planting are not invasive species that could spread from your yard to the neighboring ecosystem. To support balance, then, be mindful about adding something that may invade the local ecosystem and about taking away an existing species that may be keeping others in check. (See Resources section for a website on invasive species.)

The key to balance is organic

Chemical pesticides, and to some extent chemical fertilizers, kill the micro-organisms that ensure your plants get fed. In fact, any potent substance, organic or not, that kills insects, weeds, fungi, rodents and algae will also harm other beings in the system. The key to a healthy, balanced ecosystem is to enhance the micro-organisms in your soil and on your plants, not kill them off. So it is wise to use only organic products that sustain life in your eco-yard. Compost and actively aerated compost tea are effective tools to build micro-organic life. (See Chapter 9, The Wonders of Compost.)

DIVERSITY

Diversity—a collection of many different species—is important to a healthy ecosystem. When many species take up niches and play their various roles in an ecosystem, more support is available to all. It's like organizing a large event: it takes a number of people playing a number of roles (event planners, hotel staff, transportation support, printing staff for the invitations and menus, etc.)—the more varied the roles, the better the support for the event. It's often easier to organize and stage an event in a large city because there are many people in each niche who can do the job. By contrast, in a small town, individuals must often take on more than one role, filling several niches. This can be taxing for both the individual and the organizational group. Worse, if that person must give up their role, without a replacement the whole system is weakened.

Diversity is also important should conditions of the ecosystem change. If conditions no longer support particular species that play certain roles, those species can die off, allowing others to take over those

A Little Talk About the Birds and the Bees

How exactly do plants make more plants? Plants reproduce in many ways. More than half reproduce sexually via pollination, which happens when pollen (containing plant sperm or male genes) enters a plant's pistil or ovary (female part of plant). Some plants have both male and female parts, either in the same flowers, or in different flowers or cones. Plants that are only male or only female, such as poplars, are known as dioecious plants.

Some plants, such as the common poppy shown opposite, are self-pollinating—the male parts can fertilize the female parts on the same flower or elsewhere on the same plant. Others need cross-pollination, which happens when pollen from one plant's stamen travels to a separate plant's stigma. Cross-pollination is important for genetic diversity in a species.

Many plants require help—from the wind or from pollinators such as insects (including bees and butterflies), hummingbirds and even bats. When a pollinator comes to plants to sip nectar or collect pollen, some pollen sticks to it. When the pollinator then visits another plant, the pollen is carried to the second plant where it rubs off, thus cross-pollinating it. Flowers have evolved to specific shapes, colors and scents that attract specific pollinators. For example, some plants feature a little platform for the pollinator. Trumpet-shaped flowers attract humming-birds. So do red, pink and orange flowers—visible from far away.

Do you like to eat apples, blueberries, strawberries, almonds, melons, peaches or pumpkins? Then you have a serious interest in preserving pollinators and their habitats.

niches or roles. With a wide variety of species, a number of backup species can fill in as needed. If you have only one lead soprano for an opera and she loses her voice, without a second trained and ready to fill in, the whole performance is in jeopardy. Similarly, an ecosystem can crash if vital roles are left unfilled.

In Ireland in the 1800s, people depended on a single food crop—potatoes. The potato plants were all of one type, with very little genetic diversity. When a potato blight was introduced from elsewhere and the weather conditions were right for the blight to thrive, all the

Did You Know?

- Cone-bearing plants (such as pine) produce pollen that travels on the wind from a male cone to a female cone of the same species, perhaps on the same tree.
- Hummingbirds need to eat twice their weight in nectar every day.
- Butterflies have taste cells on their feet.
- Two human activities in particular have had a major impact on pollination patterns: clearing farmland and later abandoning the same land.
- Bird, bat and bee populations have declined because of pesticide use and habitat fragmentation.
- Plants have co-evolved with their pollinators, so many species of plants have only one specific insect or other creature that pollinates them.
- 75% of the world's flowering plants depend on pollinators.
- More than 90 food crops eaten in North America depend on pollinators.

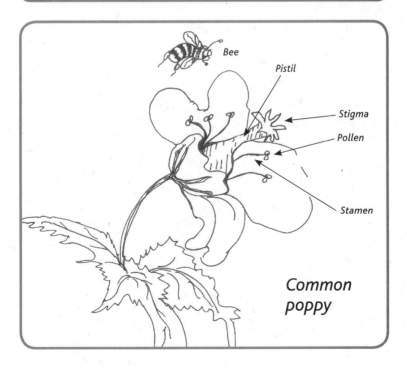

Common poppy

potatoes were susceptible. The potatoes rotted, and more than ten percent of the people died during the famine that resulted. In the 1970s, corn crops of all the same type were wiped out by a fungus in the United States, and in the following decade in California, grapes of all the same type were devastated by an insect pest.[1]

Our eco-yards can play a role in restoring diversity in our neighborhood or regional ecosystem. Native plants (ones that naturally grow in that area or region) may have been removed by developments such as housing, farmland or roads. In our eco-yards we can grow native plants or hardy plants (those that grow well in the region) that can fill the same niches as native plants. These provide food to the local pollinators (usually insects such as bees and butterflies) and often the local birds and wildlife. All of this supports the natural ecosystem of the area.

CO-CREATION WITH NATURE

An eco-yard with a rich, diverse, healthy, organic ecosystem that enriches and supports the natural ecosystem of the region and the Earth—how best to design and steward that? Copy nature! And co-create with nature in your eco-yard.

Natural Maintenance

To achieve a prairie ecosystem in an eco-yard, fire can be used in a controlled fashion every year or every second year to keep it healthy. Native prairie restoration advocates have worked with municipalities to ensure that local laws will permit this controlled burning. In some urban settings, goats and sheep are doing duty—grazing on weeds and keeping roof gardens and lawns trim.

The succession process

To understand how to co-create with nature, it's helpful to understand how plant life naturally progresses. In nature, grassed areas or meadows are usually gradually taken over by other plants in a process called succession. If the earth is disturbed, such as by a landslide or fire, first weeds will grow, then grasses and perennial flowering plants, then shrubs and then trees if conditions are right for these to grow. The ultimate stage of succession is an old-growth forest or jungle made up of large tall trees with smaller trees, shrubs, perennial flowering plants and annuals growing under them and usually vines growing on them. In areas with challenging conditions for plants, such as the arctic or the desert, the full succession process usually does not take place. Deserts and the arctic can still have plants though.

Because grass is usually replaced by shrubs and then trees, mowed lawn is rare in nature. However, fires and animals grazing and trampling are two factors that can keep areas like prairies and savannahs at the grasses stage of succession.

Here are some examples of landscape types, co-created with nature, you might find in an eco-yard:

• low-maintenance lawns of hardy grasses that require little water, mowing or added nutrition
• hardy, perennial flower beds (flowers that live over winter and bloom every year)
• woodland gardens with trees, shrubs and flowers underneath
• meadows of grasses and flowers

An eco-yard usually combines some or all of these.

In an eco-yard, the desirable plants and insects keep the undesirable ones in check. Hardy plants and grass types thrive in existing natural conditions and/or need little water. Natural wood chip or leaf mulches on flower, shrub and tree beds prevent weeds, retain moisture in the soil and add organic matter to the soil.

The Old-growth Look

Old-growth forest may be something to aspire to in an eco-yard. However, most urban residents and neighbors prefer more sun and light as well as plants that grow in the sun. Your old-growth eco-yard design could include a few large trees in areas where they allow sun and light to the house and parts of the yard.

An eco-yard may take extra labour and cost to install at first. But over the long term, eco-yards are the most environmentally and pocketbook-friendly as well as the easiest to maintain.[2]

Other types of landscapes, such as conventional lawn with annual flower beds, can be well maintained as eco-yards with the use of natural landscaping practices—it just takes a bit more up-front labour.

A VARIETY OF DESIGNS

Eco-yards can have many different features as well as unique combinations of features. A diversity of eco-yards is healthy for nature and makes the landscapes of our cities, towns and rural areas more interesting and varied.

Eco-lawns

Of the many yard features you could choose, the typical lawn of Kentucky bluegrass is the biggest user of water and chemicals and takes the most work to maintain. A key eco-yard principle is to confine lawn to just those areas where it is used for play and picnics.

> ### City Parks and Green Spaces Can Be Eco-yards
>
> City parks and green spaces can be naturalized eco-yards too! Naturalization means planting and allowing native or hardy vegetation to grow in open spaces. Urban open spaces can have mowed grass only where needed for recreation (sports, playgrounds, picnic areas, walking areas) or for access to facilities (e.g., near power poles). Areas near major roads can be planted with shrubs or hardy grasses that can be left to grow. In the long term, taxpayers save money on mowing grass, and the naturalized area will provide more habitat for beneficial insects and wildlife (imagine hearing meadowlarks or other songbirds again) and will add beauty to our urban spaces.[3] You can lobby your town and city councillors to encourage them to naturalize public spaces. To see great examples of how cities can naturalize, visit Edmonton, Alberta; Waterloo, Ontario; and Boulder, Colorado.

I've found that many people aren't quite ready to let go of their lawns, or maybe they have a space where grass is appropriate. In these cases, eco-lawns are a good alternative. An eco-lawn is made up of hardy grass types that require little water or feeding. Some of these grass types grow short and, even in towns and cities, can be left without mowing. Clover, low wildflowers or other plants can also be part of an eco-lawn.

Having an eco-lawn means getting used to grass that is a lighter green color. Letting hardy grasses go unmowed also means a more natural look. In one of my yards, I even let the Kentucky bluegrass-based grasses grow long and just mowed pathways through the lawn—I loved the look, and it was a lot less work than mowing the whole lawn!

Front yard gardens

Old practices are coming back to urban front yards (and back yards too!). For example, you could plant a vegetable garden in your front yard or a grove of aspen poplar trees. You might plant perennial flowers, shrubs and trees in your yard. A low, colorful look of flowering groundcover plants (yes, you can get varieties that grow, even in places like Calgary!) is another possibility for your eco-yard. The trend is continuing toward a wonderful variety in urban landscaping.

SUSTAINABILITY

Sustainability involves thinking, imagining and caring about future life on Earth. It means that the practices you're using can be carried on from now into centuries in the future and will sustain life on Earth. In other words, sustainable practices provide ongoing support and nurturance for life.

Most current conventional landscaping and farming practices epitomize a non-sustainable approach. Everything that grows naturally is killed by chemicals, excavating or tilling, then replaced with plants that often don't grow well in that locale. To stimulate growth, these plants are fed artificial chemical food and chlorinated water, which just leads to more need for more added resources. There definitely are better ways!

Logs used for a raised vegetable bed

Log slices from trees cut by arborist used for a pathway

Sustainable materials

Not only should the methods of maintaining the eco-yard be sustainable, so too should the materials and their sources.

A sustainable material is one whose collection, manufacture and use sustains life. Plastic is an example of a non-sustainable material, at least the plastic that is currently made from non-renewable petroleum and manufactured with the use of non-renewable energy. Petroleum-based plastic also does not biodegrade and ends up in landfills, which are usually not a sustainable solution to garbage.

An example of a sustainable material is wood chips made from prunings—tree branches that have been removed from a tree. Instead of going to a landfill, the chips go in your yard as mulch around plants to retain moisture. I prefer chips from arborists to chips from lumber mills as the lumber may not have been harvested from the forest in a sustainable way (e.g., by selective logging, in which only some trees from an area are removed).

Another example of a sustainable material is local rock that has been excavated to make way for development. This rock can be used for walls or walkways. Using local rock is more sustainable than using rock imported from far away because of the transport factor. Landscaping rock is being shipped around the world now, crossing the seas from

No Need for Landfills

In the early 1980s, I lived in a village in the jungle in Kalimantan, Indonesia. The people there threw out refuse, all of which consisted of natural materials, in their back yards. There it would be eaten by pigs and other animals, and the manure would quickly biodegrade and become compost. Food was wrapped in banana leaves for sale or transport. Plastic bags and containers were just coming into use, and it was obvious this was going to become a problem. The village had never needed a landfill for so-called trash because everything had biodegraded as part of the natural cycle. Unfortunately, bits of bright blue plastic were beginning to be scattered behind the houses.

countries such as India to North America. Trucks, trains and ships mostly use petroleum, a non-renewable resource that creates pollution and greenhouse gases. A material can be considered more sustainable when it requires less transport.

Designing for sustainability

An eco-yard can be designed to support sustainability. For example, strategically placed trees can cool a building in summer and still allow winter sun to warm it. This cuts down on pollution associated with cooling and heating.

By growing food in your yard, you avoid food transport and therefore reduce pollution and resource use. Another way to support sustainability is to choose plants that require little extra water or care in your ecosystem.

Sustainable maintenance

Sustainable maintenance practices include

• minimal or no use of gas-powered or electric machinery
• spreading compost and spraying actively aerated compost tea rather than using chemical fertilizers

SUMMARY

• An ideal eco-yard enhances and restores the natural ecosystem, locally and globally.
• Co-creating with nature is a guide to designing eco-yards.
• Minimizing lawn area is a key design principle for eco-yards.
• Use sustainable materials and design to minimize non-renewable resources use.
• Each eco-yard can be unique—diversity is great!
• An eco-yard can be an ideal to work toward—it can be co-created step-by-step over time.

NOTES

1. "Monoculture and the Irish Potato Famine: Cases of missing genetic variation," *Understanding Evolution*, evolution.berkeley.edu/evolibrary/article/_0_0/agriculture_02.

2. Jean-Marc Daigle, *Residential Landscapes: Comparison of Maintenance Costs, Time and Resources*. Commissioned by Canada Mortage and Housing Corporation (Ottawa: Government of Canada, 2000). Available only in print—a copy can be requested free by calling the CMHC library at 1-800-668-2642. This study followed 30 gardens in southern Ontario over two years—with seven different landscape types. All inputs were tracked. The study also included hypothetical designs of seven types of gardens and the costs to install and maintain them over a ten-year cycle. A literature review was also part of the study. You can read about low-maintenance lawns at cmhc-schl.gc.ca/en/co/maho/la/la_004.cfm.

3. The Coalition for a Healthy Calgary website at healthycalgary.ca has a good section on how city green spaces can be naturalized. It includes lots of examples of areas where naturalization has been successful. Waterloo, Ontario, and Boulder, Colorado, also have good websites. You can link to them from healthycalgary.ca.

3

Why Eco-yards?

If the world is going to be saved, gardeners will be the ones who do it. — Des Kennedy

Ciliates

The way we have been landscaping in the Western world has taken a toll on our health and the environment. This chapter details the main reasons why this is so and why landscaping the eco-yards way is healthier for all and more kind to the Earth.

TO COME INTO RIGHT RELATIONSHIP WITH THE EARTH

The Earth could continue without humans. Whether or not humans and a lot of other beautiful species will continue to live on Earth is another question. The answer depends on whether we humans come to right relationship with the Earth—our planet and all the beings on it—through our actions. By right relationship I mean a mutually beneficial relationship.

One action we can take toward right relationship with the Earth is to move toward having eco-yards in the plots of land we steward. These eco-yards can be in harmony with the global ecosystem.

TO PROTECT AND RESTORE THE NATURAL ENVIRONMENT

To live in harmony with all the other beings in the ecosystem of Earth, we need to steward our yards in ways that will sustain this harmony for the long term—meaning forever! By the use of natural landscaping practices, eco-yards can be maintained for centuries into the future, continuing to support and enhance the ecosystem. Eco-yards are doable and usually less work than the typical Western yard too! It's a winning scenario for all of us. The whole eco-yards movement gives me great hope that we can have beauty and sustainability in our urban landscapes.

WHAT NEEDS TO CHANGE

Much of the landscaping in the Western world today is not sustainable. Designs often include plants (like lawns) that require lots of watering and fertilizer. Yards typically do not let rain soak into the ground to restore underground water tables. Materials used in installing yards may include poor topsoils, valuable agricultural topsoils now no longer used for growing food or rocks brought from across the world at a high cost to the environment from both the quarrying and the pollution caused by shipping. Maintaining yards often involves heavy use of fertilizers and pesticides as well as gas- or electric-powered equipment that causes air, water and noise pollution.

What Is a Pesticide?

By pesticide I mean a synthetic chemical substance used to control "pests." This includes herbicides (for killing plants), insecticides (for killing insects), fungicides (for controlling fungus on plants), rodenticides (for killing rodents) and algaecides (for killing algae in ponds and streams). Some synthetic derivatives of natural substances, such as pyrethrins, are not considered to have harmful side effects, when used properly, and are considered among natural pesticides.

TO RESTORE THE SOIL—
THE FOUNDATION OF LIFE

The chemical and mechanical practices (tilling) used in agriculture and landscaping over the last 100 years have depleted the life-giving part of soil, the organic matter and micro-organisms.[1] Healthy soil is the foundation of life on Earth because plants need healthy soil to grow and everything else needs (eats) plants. So it would definitely be wise to change these practices. Restoring soil health is the foundation of a good eco-yard. Healthy, ecologically rich urban gardens can be important storehouses for critical soil micro-organisms that may be helpful in restoring agricultural soils elsewhere. (For more on the importance of soil, see Chapter 8, Soil: A Feeding Frenzy.)

Soil micro-organisms: predatory nematode, bacteria, flagellate

What does "restore" mean?

By "restore" I mean working with the soil, plants, insects and other living beings on Earth to create a healthy, productive ecosystem that supports abundant life. We have the know-how now to co-create, with other living beings, landscapes that can surpass most of what has existed before on Earth in terms of the amount of food and number of flowers grown in a given space.

Restoration here does not mean going back to some pristine state that may have existed at some point in the past. Humans have been shaping landscapes and been shaped by them since we emerged on Earth. While it is probable that many cultures have and have had great ecological wisdom, very often they simply operated on a scale that was not so widely destructive. The environment could recover from practices such as slash-and-burn agriculture (cutting some forest and burning it, planting and harvesting a crop and then moving on to cut down the next piece of forest).

There is evidence some civilizations collapsed because they did not manage their agricultural land and practices to sustain their populations. Two of these are the Sumerians, who lived in Mesopotamia (now Iraq), and the Mayans in Mesoamerica (now Central America). The Sumerians exploited the land, leaving it vulnerable to flooding and erosion. Extensive irrigation to support intensified production resulted in salinization. By 2000 BC the earth had turned white with salt, crops failed and previously wealthy cities were abandoned. Sumeria became effectively extinct. (Today half of Iraq's land is saline.) In the ninth century AD, Mayan civilization collapsed when the land was pushed beyond its limit by overpopulation, urbanization, destruction of the rainforest and fields worn out from intensive farming.[2]

Humans are a part of Earth's ecosystem. We have the capacity now to have a huge influence, and it would be prudent to make this influence healthy and sustainable for the long term.

TO RESTORE WATER RESOURCES

Restoring underground water tables

Much of the water we humans use for agriculture and for our yards is drawn from underground water sources. These aquifers are replenished when rainwater or snowmelt soaks back into the ground. In towns and cities, much of the land is covered with roads, buildings, parking lots and lawn. These features don't absorb water nearly as readily as a natural landscape does. Hard surfaces don't absorb water at all; the water runs into gutters and storm sewers, and usually the untreated water eventually reaches streams and rivers. Lawn, with less than ten percent of the absorptive capacity of a woodland landscape (e.g., tree, shrub, flower beds covered with organic mulch such as wood chips), also contributes to runoff.[3] This is one reason mulched beds are recommended for eco-yards.

Eco-yards can be designed and maintained to use and absorb the water that drains from building roofs and falls on the yard itself.

Eco-yards can also be designed to need little if any watering. (See Chapter 11, Water-wise Design.)

During my spring 2008 visit to Portland, Oregon, friends told me that the City of Portland's storm sewers tie in with the sanitary sewers before the water is treated. When there is too much runoff, the sewers get overloaded and both the raw sewage and storm water runoff gets dumped into the Columbia River. The City is now building two separate systems for sewage and storm water runoff. Meanwhile, school children are going house to house to place downspouts from house roofs to drain into the yards so that less water goes into the storm water sewer system.

In Calgary, where I live, the City encourages use of rain barrels and downspouts draining into yards so that people use less municipally treated water for their yards.

Consider that Portland has too much water and Calgary too little for its overall water needs, and yet both cities promote similar eco-yard methods as solutions.

Preserving water resources

Using water wisely is another reason for eco-yards. On average, 40 to 70 percent of municipally treated water in North America is used on landscapes. Municipalities have been working together across North America since the 1980s and '90s to promote water-wise landscaping, both to make better use of tax dollars and preserve water resources.

Restoring health to waterways and groundwater

Typically, a large percentage of the chemical pesticides and fertilizers used on urban yards washes off into gutters, sewers and then into waterways when it rains or when yards are watered. These chemicals can be destructive to the ecosystem of life (fish, plants, insects) in those waterways.

Pesticides are also then found in the drinking water of those downstream from urban centers. While the pesticide levels rarely exceed what is thought to be harmful to human health, Alberta scientist Anne-Marie Anderson writes, "There are uncertainties about how comprehensively pesticide risk in surface waters can be assessed using current guidelines."[4]

Underground water (or groundwater) can also have high levels of pesticides and salts from fertilizers—high enough that, in some places where fertilizers are used heavily for agriculture, farm families avoid drinking their own well water.[5]

> ### Pesticides in Urban Streams and Irrigation Canals
>
> In a U.S. government survey carried out between 1992 and 2001, 83 percent of urban streams were found to have levels of pesticides that exceeded a level considered safe for aquatic life.[6] A 2005 survey of pesticide monitoring in Alberta surface water found the pesticide index was worst for irrigation canals and urban streams, with over 75 percent of those having poor to marginal levels.[7]

Eco-yards support preserving the life in our beautiful streams, rivers and oceans and preserving the health and abundance of our underground water.

READ ON IF YOU NEED MORE MOTIVATION TO ADOPT NATURAL LANDSCAPING PRACTICES

Carry on with reading this chapter if, in order to be motivated to change your ways, you need to know more about the harm chemical landscaping practices cause. If you are already convinced, you may want to skip to Chapter 4.

Why skip the rest of this chapter? Sometimes focusing on the way things are now can cause us to get stuck in despair and lose motivation. Sometimes we can get caught up in the way things are now rather than working on creating healthier ways to live on the Earth in the future. Also, we need to keep our motivation in order to take action, such as lobbying politicians to pass laws that phase out pesticide use or ban sales of pesticides. In her books and workshops, Joanna Macy (*Despair and Personal Power in the Nuclear Age* and *World As Lover, World As*

Self) says we need to deeply feel that despair that we may have for ourselves, other living beings on the planet and future generations and to realize that we would not feel that despair unless we cared deeply about life. The despair comes from our love. Macy offers processes that help people move through their despair (and the only way is through it!) by focusing on their love for the world and their vision for its future. The critical last step in these processes is taking action to manifest the vision.[8]

The most effective way to create a world of eco-yards is to hold a positive vision of what that would look, feel, sound, taste and smell like and to take creative steps toward working with the soil, the plants, the other beings in your yard and your neighbors, to support and enrich the symphony of life.

So read on in this chapter if you are ready to work through what may come up for you emotionally and are willing to focus on hopeful visions and carry them through to positive action.

TO PROTECT HUMAN HEALTH

The weight of scientific evidence shows strong relationships between pesticide use and many human health challenges, including those related to cell mutations, neurological difficulties, learning challenges, birth defects and disruption of hormone function.

When humans are developing and growing, from the fetal stages to teen years, they are particularly at risk of having that development disrupted by synthetic pesticides.

Humans are exposed to pesticides through

- breathing them in during application or from the air. Pesticides can drift far in the wind and can evaporate for up to weeks after application.
- skin contact when applying pesticides or in brushing against plants such as grass on which there are pesticides.
- contact with pesticides that have been tracked into buildings on shoes. Some pesticides can persist for up to a year inside.
- accidentally eating or drinking them. Most commonly, children may

eat grass or put in their mouths toys that have pesticide residue
on them.
•pre-natal exposure. Babies are exposed when their parents are
exposed. Yes, there is some evidence that sperm is affected by
pesticides.

The many, precise ways in which pesticides affect human health have
not yet been determined. It is difficult to isolate the effects of pesticide
exposure from other environmental factors that might affect health.
Even so, scientists worldwide say we have enough evidence to show
that pesticides cause harm. Scientists are urging that the *precautionary
principle* be used:

> When an activity raises threats of harm to human health or the
> environment, precautionary measures should be taken even if
> some cause-and-effect relationships are not fully established
> scientifically.[9]

The only way to exactly determine how pesticides affect human health
would be to test pesticides on humans. However, it would be unethical
to administer pesticides to humans when we know the pesticides are
probably harmful and there is no health benefit (as there may be in
drug trials).

Meanwhile, the American Medical Association has suggested that
"homeowners, farmers, and workers limit pesticide exposure to
themselves and others" and consider using "the least toxic chemical
pesticides or nonchemical alternatives."[10] Many medical bodies,
including the Ontario College of Family Physicians, the Canadian
Association of Physicians for the Environment, the Registered Nurses
Association of Ontario and the Canadian Cancer Society, support
phasing out the cosmetic use of pesticides (that is, using pesticides
simply to make lawns and gardens look nice) altogether.

The Supreme Court of Canada has twice upheld the right of
municipalities to pass bylaws phasing out the use of cosmetic
pesticides. (These would be ordinances in the United States.) Indeed,
the Supreme Court and the federal Minister of Health at that time
recommended such bylaws as a complement to federal regulation of
pesticides. The opposite has happened in the U.S.!

Pesticide Laws: Protection vs. Preemption

In the United States, some municipalities passed local ordinances restricting pesticide use as early as the 1980s, but many of these ordinances were subsequently overturned. On its website, the Beyond Pesticides coalition explains:

Currently, California and 40 other states have pesticide "preemption" laws that deny local authorities the right to pass pesticide restrictions that are more stringent than the state's laws. Preemption laws are a result of intensive lobbying by the agrichemical industry, and groups in California and across the country believe the time has come to take back the democratic right for localities to adopt restrictions to protect environmental and public health. This authority enables local jurisdictions to respond to exposure scenarios that are not addressed by state law and address unique contamination or poisoning situations....

Realizing that federal and state pesticide regulations are often not strong enough to protect public health and the environment, and do not take into account local environmental or health issues, many towns, cities, and counties have been passing non-toxic landscape care policies, and school integrated pest management (IPM) policies. With preemption laws in place, however, these policies can only extend as far as government-owned property, and do not restrict the use of toxic chemicals for homeowners.[11]

Local authorities, particularly in California and New York, are now beginning to challenge the preemption laws. City-wide pesticide bans may again be possible before long. In the meantime, many U.S. cities are finding ways to reduce pesticide use.[12]

Don't government regulations protect us? Sadly, not enough! You may ask: If pesticides are unnecessary and harmful, why haven't government regulating agencies taken them off the market?

In Canada, the mandate of the Pest Management Regulatory Agency (PMRA) is to register pesticides for use if studies submitted by the pesticide companies show that the probability of risk to human health and to the environment is "acceptable" (below a defined level according to animal studies and other studies, not studies on humans) and that the product does what it is advertised to do (that is, it kills the target species).

While products usually use a combination of pesticides in order to be more lethal, most of the tests are done on one pesticide ingredient only. Moreover, most of the testing does not include the binders, solvents and wetting agents that represent up to 90 percent of pesticide formulations. These are just some of the examples of how the science used by government regulation agencies is inadequate to ensure protection of our health and the environment.

Registration by the PMRA does not mean that a pesticide is safe. In fact, the Pest Control Products Act prohibits advertising pesticides as safe. Remember, the federal government regulates the sale of cigarettes too! The situation is similar with the Environmental Protection Agency in the United States.

The Doctor Is In

It is not a case of innocent until proven guilty. We have ample reason to be concerned. We must act on what we know now, because health risks are cumulative and can last for years.

— Dr. J. Reisman, Chief of Paediatrics, Children's Hospital of Eastern Ontario; Professor and Chairman, Department of Paediatrics, Faculty of Medicine, University of Ottawa[13]

The office of the Auditor General of Canada released a report in 2003 concluding that "the federal government is not managing pesticides effectively.... The range of weaknesses raises serious questions about the overall management of the health and environmental risks associated with pesticides."[14] While the PMRA is improving, its registration process is still not adequate to protect us from the effects of pesticide use.

Pesticides are not necessary to beautiful lawns and gardens. In fact, using chemicals only results in the need for more inputs. Using organic

Cosmetic Pesticides Banned in Provinces and Municipalities

The provinces of Quebec and Ontario have banned the sale and use of "the most toxic" cosmetic pesticides! Quebec's Pesticides Management Code, phased in from 2003 to 2006, regulates the sale, storage and use of pesticides. Among other provisions, it prohibits the use, for lawn maintenance, of 13 active ingredients (insecticides, herbicides and fungicides) including the weedkiller 2,4-D. This ban has now been extended to commercial and private property (except golf courses).[15]

As of January 2009, 152 Canadian municipalities have passed bylaws to phase out the use of cosmetic pesticides, including Toronto, Vancouver and Halifax.

The Good News

The good news is that there is some evidence that reducing use of pesticides does improve health statistics. Two pesticides associated with the cancer non-Hodgkin lymphoma were banned in Sweden in the late 1970s. Twenty years later, studies showed that the rates among the general population were down![16]

eco-yard methods is healthier for our yard, the Earth, our children, neighbors—all of us.[17]

TO PROTECT THE HEALTH AND WELL-BEING OF PETS AND WILDLIFE

Pets and wildlife can be exposed to pesticides in many ways:

• Their skin, coats and feet absorb pesticides from grass or other plants.
• They ingest pesticides when grooming and licking their coat or skin.
• They eat pesticide granules, pesticide-treated plants, insects or other animals poisoned by pesticides.
• They breathe pesticides in the air and drink pesticides in water.

Concentrations of persistent pesticides increase in wildlife that are higher on the food chain.[18] Birds especially have been affected by pesticides—one estimate is that 67 million birds die annually in the United States from pesticide exposure.[19] Long-term exposure to pesticides also decreases bird reproduction.[20]

Using organic products in our eco-yards is healthier for our pets and wildlife. Eco-yards can also provide food and shelter—a habitat for wildlife—in our urban yards and green spaces.

A warbler

istockphoto.com/Andrew Howe

A monarch butterfly sipping nectar from a meadow blazingstar (liatris)

TO PROTECT AND RESTORE BENEFICIAL INSECTS

Most of our vegetables, trees and flowers rely on insects to spread pollen amongst them so they can reproduce. Experts are warning that we may be coming to a crisis in our food supply with not enough pollinating insects to keep agricultural plants reproducing. City dwellers can help by having a diversity of flowering plants and trees in their yards to provide habitat and food for pollinating insects.

A healthy, diverse insect population keeps all insect species in balance. Insects like ladybugs and praying mantises eat destructive insects like aphids. Insects also provide food for birds and wildlife and help to decompose natural litter from animals and plants.

Natural landscaping practices allow ladybugs, bees, butterflies and other beneficial insects to flourish and spread more beauty and nourishment. Pesticides kill these beneficial insects.

Did You Know?

- One ladybug can eat 5,000 aphids in its lifetime.
- One dragonfly can eat 300 mosquitoes in a day.
- One lacewing larva can eat 60 aphids in an hour.[21]

FOR BEAUTY

Our souls are fed by natural beauty. Seeing, smelling, tasting, hearing, feeling and sensing pleasing sights, scents, sounds, textures and energy can exalt us.

Having eco-yards that delight us and our neighbors can enrich and sustain our spirits, adding more joy and peace to our lives.

Imagine the Influence

In Canada, 70 percent of adults garden and eight million households have yards. Canadians spend about $3 billion per year on yard-related goods and services. In the United States, about 30 trillion acres and $45 billion annually are devoted to American lawns—more than is spent on agriculture. What North Americans spend on their yards annually is about the equivalent of the annual budget of India. This is a lot of people power and money. Imagine the influence on the Earth if these resources were put toward eco-yards. Once installed, eco-yards are inexpensive to maintain. We'd have a huge heap of dollars left for other purposes.[22]

SUMMARY

Why should we choose eco-yards?

• to enhance environmental sustainability
• to restore the natural ecosystem
  (soil, plants, beneficial insects, birds, wildlife, water)
• to protect human health
• to protect pets and wildlife
• for beauty

Moving toward a world of eco-yards is simply the smart thing to do. Future generations may wonder why we didn't do this sooner.

NOTES

1. It takes approximately 100 years to naturally generate one millimeter of soil. University of Michigan, "Land Degradation," globalchange.umich.edu/globalchange2/current/lectures/land_deg/land_deg.html.

   In the U.S. Midwest, about half the organic matter in soils "has been lost since the land was first cultivated." The University of Illinois started measuring this in 1876 on the Morrow Test Plots, cultivating agricultural crops. Even with "high fertility levels and constant cropping," organic matter levels in the plots have declined from 4.9% to 2.2%. This is largely due to frequent tilling which speeds up the breakdown of organic matter, converting it into carbon dioxide that releases into the air. Dan Towery, "Organic Matter, the Essence of Soil Quality," *Agronomy Notes* 46 (Montana State University, 1995–1996), agnotes.org/AgNotes/docs/46. htm, summarized from a newsletter of the Conservation Technology Information Center (West Lafayette, IN).

There is also evidence that intensive agricultural use of nitrogen fertilizers led to the decline in carbon (organic matter) in the Morrow plots and elsewhere. S.A. Khan et al., "The Myth of Nitrogen Fertilization for Soil Carbon Sequestration," *Journal of Environmental Quality* 36, no. 6 (2007): 1821–32.

Levels of organic matter in Canadian agricultural soils are now increasing or staying even, soil structure is improving and less land is being salinized. D. F. Acton and L. J. Gregorich, eds., *The Health of Our Soils: Towards Sustainable Agriculture in Canada*, Agriculture and Agri-Food Canada Publication 1906/E (Ottawa: Center for Land and Biological Research, 1995), xiii, 40, 45, referred to by Laura Jones et al., *Environmental Indicators*, 4th ed., Critical Issues Bulletin (Vancouver: The Fraser Institute, 2000), indicator 4, "Land," oldfraser.lexi.net/ publications/critical_issues/2000/env_indic/section_06.html.

2. Ronald Wright, *A Short History of Progress* (Toronto: House of Anansi Press, 2004), chapters 2 and 3. These Massey lectures, originally broadcast on CBC Radio, are also available on audio CD.

3. United States Environmental Protection Agency, "Beneficial Landscaping," epa.gov/greenkit/landscap.htm.

4. Anne-Marie Anderson explains the uncertainties: "There are uncertainties about how comprehensively pesticide risk in surface waters can be assessed using current guidelines. These uncertainties stem from the unavailability of guidelines for over half of the pesticides detected in Alberta surface waters, the fact that guidelines apply to single compounds, and that many samples have multiple pesticide occurrences or multiple incidences of non-compliance." Anne-Marie Anderson, "Overview of Pesticide Data in Alberta Surface Waters Since 1995" (Environmental Monitoring and Evaluation Branch, Alberta

Environment, November 2005), www3.gov.ab.ca/env/water/reports/
PesticideData_SurfaceWatersSince1995.pdf.

5. D.C. Gosselin et al., "Domestic Well Water Quality in Rural Nebraska:
Focus on Nitrate-Nitrogen, Pesticides, and Coliform Bacteria," *Ground
Water Monitoring & Remediation* 17, no. 2 (Spring 1997): 77–87; Kira
Jacobs, "Private Well Contamination Adjacent to a Vermont Farm:
A Case Study of Collaboration Between Federal, State, Agricultural,
and Residential Partners" (paper presented at a conference of the
Groundwater Foundation, Nebraska City, NE, November 3, 2005),
groundwater.org/gi/docs/2005whitepapers.pdf.

6. United States Department of the Interior, U.S. Geological Survey,
Fact Sheet 2006-3028. "Pesticides in the Nation's Streams and
Ground Water. 1992–2001, A Summary,"
pubs.water.usgs.gov/fs20063028.

7. For source, see end of Note 4.

8. Joanna Macy, *Despair and Personal Power in the Nuclear Age*
(Philadelphia: New Society Publishers, 1983), and *World As Lover,
World As Self: Courage for Global Justice and Ecological Renewal*
(Berkeley: Parallax Press, 2007).
See her website at joannamacy.net.

9. "The Wingspread Consensus Statement on the Precautionary
Principle" (Wingspread Conference on the Precautionary Principle,
Racine, WI, January 26, 1998),
sehn.org/wing.html.

10. The American Medical Association met in 1994 to discuss the concerns
over pesticide use, and this is the link to the actual report from their
meeting: ama-assn.org/ama1/pub/upload/mm/443/csai-94.pdf. Scroll to
page 7 for the details.

11. "California Bill to Reestablish Local Control of Pesticides," *Beyond
Pesticides Daily News Blog*, posted July 21, 2008,
beyondpesticides.org/dailynewsblog/.

12. For the latest news on pesticide regulation in the U.S., see the websites
of the Beyond Pesticides coalition at

beyondpesticides.org and Pesticide Action Network North America at panna.org.

13. J. Reisman, "Ottawa Experts Call for Pesticide-free Landscaping," The Coalition for a Healthy Ottawa, flora.org/healthyottawa/experts.htm.

14. Office of the Auditor General of Canada, "Managing the Safety and Accessibility of Pesticides," chapter 1 in *Report of the Commissioner of the Environment and Sustainable Development to the House of Commons* (Ottawa: Minister of Public Works and Government Services Canada, 2003), oag-bvg.gc.ca/internet/docs/c20031001ce.pdf.

15. These two pages on the website of Quebec's Ministère du Développement durable, de l'Environnement et des Parcs explain the Pesticides Management Code in English: mddep.gouv.qc.ca/pesticides/permis-en/code -gestion-en/index.htm and mddep.gouv.qc.ca/pesticides/permis-en/ code-gestion-en/municipal/index.htm.

16. Lennart Hardell and Mikael Eriksson, "Is the Decline of the Increasing Incidence of Non-Hodgkin Lymphoma in Sweden and Other Countries a Result of Cancer Preventive Measures?" *Environmental Health Perspectives* 111 (2003): 1704–06. Two pesticides—phenoxyacetic acids and chlorophenols—that have been associated with non-Hodgkin lymphoma were banned in Sweden in the late 1970s. Other persistent organic pollutants (e.g., PCBs) also linked to non-Hodgkin lymphoma had their highest use in the 1960s and 1970s. The decline of the rate of occurrence among the general population of non-Hodgkin lymphoma in Sweden and some other countries shows that prohibiting the use of these chemicals may have a positive health effect that shows up in statistics decades later. The non-Hodgkin lymphoma rate in Sweden increased by 3.2% among men and 3.1% among women from 1971 to 1990. From 1991 to 2000, the rate for men went down by 0.8%, and for women it decreased by 0.2%.

17. Go to my website eco-yards.com for much more explanation of why federal regulations don't protect us and much more information on the health effects associated with pesticide use, including summaries of health studies and links to health studies. That information is elsewhere so that this book's emphasis is on positive, visionary, hopeful solutions.

18. AG Care, "Do Pesticides Build up in the Bodies of Animals?" *Agriculture Pesticide Facts*, agcare.org/File
.aspx?id=d43fc777-b5ed-4d06-8b89-8fd328f8aed9.

19. D. Pimentel et al., "The Environmental and Economic Costs of Pesticide Use," *BioScience* 42 (1992): 750–60.

20. American Bird Conservancy, "Pesticides and Birds,"
.abcbirds.org/abcprograms/policy/pesticides/; P.S.C. Rao et al., *Pesticides and Their Behavior in Soil and Water*, Soil Science Fact Sheet (Florida Cooperative Extension Service, Institute of Food and Agricultural Sciences, University of Florida, 1983).

21. *A Kid's Guide to Backyard Bugs* (City and County of San Francisco, 1999), mywatershedwatch.org/pdf_files/KidsGuide.pdf.

22. The Canadian statistics come from *Tending the Earth: A Gardener's Manifesto* by Lorraine Johnson (Toronto: Penguin, 2002), 161.

The U.S. statistics come from a video on buildinggreentv.com called "Eco-friendly Yards: Landscaping Using Water-wise Plants and Creating Natural Habitats". I watched it on Feb. 22, 2008.

The landscaping cost comparison comes from Jean-Marc Daigle, *Residential Landscapes: Comparison of Maintenance Costs, Time and Resources*, commissioned by the Canada Mortgage and Housing Corporation (Ottawa: Government of Canada, 2000). Available only in print—a copy can be requested free by calling the CMHC library at 1-800-668-2642.

The comparison with the budget of India I heard on CBC Radio a few years ago in a talk given by anthropologist Wade Davis.

4

Eco-maintenance

Without wildness, we lose our humanness. We need the weeds at the edges of our gardens. —Trevor Herriot

Bacteria-eating nematode

You can maintain your current yard in an Earth-friendly manner, whether it's an eco-yard or not. Eco-maintenance means using practices that support the natural ecosystem, especially the all-important micro-organisms that ensure your plants get fed.

KEEP YOUR YARD HEALTHY AND BEAUTIFUL— NATURALLY!

Copy nature in your yard design and you will usually find your yard requires less maintenance. It will also better support the natural ecosystem. This usually means replacing lawn with shrubs, trees and flowerbeds (see Chapter 10, Designing Your Eco-yard). Where lawn is a good choice, you can gradually replace your existing grass by overseeding with native grasses (see Chapter 6, What's in a Lawn?).

In maintaining your yard, refrain from using chemicals or potent organic solutions. Make sure any landscaping service provider you hire uses truly organic products. Provide food to your plants naturally by using compost and actively aerated compost tea. Use natural mulches, such as wood chips and leaves, on your beds to prevent weeds, retain moisture and add organic matter to the soil. Grass clippings left on your lawn will feed your lawn.

Apartment and Condo Dwellers Can Have Eco-yards Too!

If you live or work in an apartment or rental property, talk to your landlord about using natural landscaping practices. If you live in a condominium complex, bring up using natural landscaping practices with your condo board. Many condos are going green! I now offer three- and four-year green plans for condos that include replacing lawn with tree, shrub and flower beds, replacing the remaining lawn areas with hardier grass types and spraying actively aerated compost tea on their grounds.

Go for a more natural look to save labour, costs and non-renewable resources. Let grass grow long where it's a challenge to clip it, and accept some weeds. Use manual equipment as much as possible.

SPREAD COMPOST GENEROUSLY

Topdressing—spreading compost (decomposed organic matter) on your lawn and around your flowers, trees and shrubs—will add a rich system of micro-organisms to your soil and improve the ability of your soil to provide nutrition to your plants. Compost itself is also a rich fertilizer. See Chapter 8, Soil: A Feeding Frenzy, for more on why soil health through compost is the foundation of your eco-yard!

Top-dressing your beds

Spread a layer of finished compost (1 in. or 3 cm) on the soil under your flowers, trees and shrubs. You can do this regularly. If you have mulch on your beds, it is best to pull back the mulch (a rake is the ideal tool for this), spread the compost and then spread the mulch back over top of the compost. If you cannot pull back the mulch, just put your compost on top of it. The nutrients and micro-organisms will still find their way into the soil—it just may take a little longer.

Top-dressing your lawn

Spreading a thin layer of compost (½ in. or 1 cm) will liven up your lawn so it will need less water and fertilizer. Top-dressing can be done anytime; it is usually done once a year in the spring. If you aerate your lawn (see below), top-dress right after aeration. The compost will go deeper into the soil as it fills in the aeration holes.

Buying compost

If you don't have your own compost, the cheapest and often easiest way to buy compost is in bulk. You can have a landscape supply company or compost company deliver compost to your yard.

Top-dressing a flower bed with compost

A load of delivered compost

You can also pick up a load of compost yourself at a landscape supply or composting facility. Most facilities will have a loader to load your pickup truck. If you don't have access to a truck, or don't need that much compost, you can take containers and load them yourself with a shovel.

Buy good quality compost that has completely finished composting. And yes, composts do vary greatly in their quality. How do you know it is good quality? Ask for copies of lab tests, especially of the soil biology.[1] Read the lab's summary about the quality. Quality compost will have lots of micro-organisms and a great diversity of micro-organisms as well as a suitable pH. Quality compost will also be low in salts.

How do you know that it has finished composting? It will smell like soil rather than manure or wood, and it will not be hot. If the compost is steaming, it is not finished, so let it sit in a pile somewhere in a corner of your yard for a few weeks to complete decomposition.

Fresh manure or unfinished manure-based compost (the compost used to grow mushrooms, for example, is usually manure and straw)

Dressing Doesn't Have to Cost the Earth

You can pay a landscaping company to top-dress your lawn, but it's much less expensive to do it yourself.

has lots of ammonia and salts and can burn or dry out plants.[2] So compost it yourself for a year before using it. If you can get it to the proper temperature (see Making Compost in Chapter 9, The Wonders of Compost), you will also kill the weed seeds that are often abundant in manure.

If you are top-dressing perennial flowers, shrubs and trees, a wood-based compost should provide the fungi needed for their healthy growth. Manure-based compost that leans to more bacteria is fine for lawns. (See Chapter 8, Soil: A Feeding Frenzy, for why this is so.)

Bulk compost is sold by the cubic meter or cubic yard. To figure out how much compost you will need, use this formula:

length (in feet) × width (in feet) × depth (in inches) ÷ 324 = cubic yards needed

For example, if you are going to spread ½ in. (1 cm) of compost on your back lawn and the lawn is 12 feet by 20 feet, you need: 12 × 20 × 0.5 ÷ 324 = 0.37 cubic yards. (Most people calculate in feet, inches and yards. Cubic meters work out to nearly the same values.) If your measurements are metric, use these formulas:

length (in meters) × width (in meters) × depth (in centimeters) × 0.013 = cubic yards needed

length (in meters) × width (in meters) × depth (in centimeters) × 0.01 = cubic meters needed

You can find an easy-to-use volume calculator on the websites of some companies that sell landscaping materials. Most urban yards need about a cubic yard or cubic meter of compost for top-dressing the lawn and beds. A pickup truck box usually holds about 1½ cubic meters or yards.

Spreading compost

You can spread the compost with a shovel, wheelbarrow and rake. Just load the wheelbarrow full of compost with your shovel and dump the compost on your lawn (you can wiggle the end of the wheelbarrow to fan the compost out). Then spread the compost with a leaf rake. Leaf rakes work well as they are light and won't dig into your lawn. I have

also used a light flat-ended scoop shovel, or the back of a regular rake, to spread compost on a lawn.

You can also use a compost spreader with a hopper. These manual spreaders cost about $1,000 to purchase; in some locations they are available for rent. If you somehow find one, make sure the compost is dry and fine so that it doesn't clump up in the spreader.

Dumping compost on a lawn

Raking out compost on a lawn

Using a compost spreader

USE ACTIVELY AERATED COMPOST TEA TO IMPROVE YARD HEALTH

Using actively aerated compost tea is the cheapest and often the easiest way to add organic matter to your yard and enhance the health of both soil and plants (see Chapter 9, The Wonders of Compost.) The tea is made by putting high-quality compost in water and pumping lots of air through it for a day. The liquid is then a rich soup of soil micro-organisms. Each time you spray compost tea on plants, shrubs, trees and soil, you increase the number of micro-organisms on the plants and in the soil. As your soil becomes richer in organic life, its ability to provide nutrients to your plants increases, as does the health of your plants.

Leaf It Onsite

Leaves from your trees are one of the most valuable resources for the health of your eco-yard. Spread them on your beds to protect plants over winter and to provide organic matter. If you have more than you need, compost them. I keep some leaves bagged year-round to add to my compost bins every time I add kitchen waste.

MAKE SURE YOUR LANDSCAPING SERVICE USES NO SYNTHETIC PESTICIDES

If you use a yard care company to fertilize your yard, ask if they have a pesticide-free option and switch to that. If they do not, hire one of the many other companies that do offer pesticide-free options. And make sure their products and services are indeed pesticide-free. Many companies will tell you that they only spot spray pesticides directly on the weeds. Ask them not to spot spray—they are still applying enough pesticide to cause harm to the environment and to human health.

The Competition Bureau of Canada is warning consumers to ask questions to determine if lawn care products really are "organic" or "environmentally friendly." Many are not. Here are just three of the questions that the bureau recommends asking potential service providers:

• Does the program include the use of chemical pesticides, even at a minimum (spot treatments)?
• If the treatment includes chemical pesticides, which ones are used and what precautions should be taken to protect children and pets?
• If the treatment claims to be "safe," what are the ingredients that eliminate weeds and are there any hazards associated with these ingredients?

For the entire set of questions to ask, see competitionbureau.gc.ca/epic/site/cb-bc.nsf/en/01154e.html.[3]

If you witness a yard care company in Canada that claims to be "green" using synthetic pesticides or that makes other claims you consider misleading, complain to the federal Competition Bureau at 1-800-348-5358 or visit their website at: competitionbureau.gc.ca.

Sometimes the Old Ways Just Work Best

In one large yard near a park, I used a small gas-powered weed whipper. Eventually I reverted to using a scythe rather than the weed whipper and just let the grass grow along the edges for a more natural look.

In the United States, contact the Federal Trade Commission Consumer Response Center at 1-866-382-4357 or ftc.gov under "Consumer Protection" and then "Environment."

USE BENIGN EQUIPMENT

Still today, most gas-powered equipment produces pollution and greenhouse gases that contribute to global warming. Even electric equipment isn't faultless—the source and method of electricity production likely produce pollution and greenhouse gases and may have other environmental impacts (e.g., dams for hydroelectricity). Landscaping equipment also makes a lot of noise.

If you have a gas lawn mower, it is best for long-term sustainability to replace it with a push mower. Many models are now available, and some retail outlets will even give you a credit for bringing in your gas

Using a push mower

> ### Mouse or Sasquatch?
> ### Calculate Your Ecological Footprint
>
> Our ecological footprint measures the demands that our lifestyle makes on our planet's resources and the waste our lifestyle produces. These are then compared to the Earth's ecological capacity. You can calculate your own ecological footprint by using one of the many footprint calculators on the Web—search for "ecological footprint calculator."

mower. Another alternative is a battery-powered recharging electric mower. However, while these use less energy than gas mowers, they still usually use non-renewable energy sources.

We now have lots of power equipment for landscaping, such as weed whippers and leaf blowers. My advice is to refrain from using the equipment—go for a natural look—let the grass grow long (or replace your grass with flowers and shrubs!) along the edges of your yards and trees. Let the leaves blow across your driveway. Use manual methods like clippers or brooms, or just let the look of your yard go more natural.

If you hire landscaping companies, ask them what they are doing to reduce their ecological footprint. Let them know it's important to you to encourage them to search out more sustainable methods.

I weigh the benefits of replacing grass with hardier grass types, spraying aerated compost tea and doing hauling that requires a truck against the emissions all this equipment uses. My vision for the future is to

> ### Taking My Own Medicine
>
> As a landscaper, I do have a truck and some gas-powered equipment. I will be converting the engines on my slit-seeder and aerated compost tea sprayer to small diesel engines for which I will use biodiesel. My next truck will be fueled by biodiesel. Currently I use Freedom Fuel International fuel pellets in all my gas engines, including my truck. These pellets are said to cut emissions by 75 percent or more and increase fuel efficiency by 7–14 percent.

consolidate my client base closer to home so I travel less, to use manual and no-equipment methods as much as I can and to continue to use the least polluting equipment I can find.

SPRING CLEANUP

If you have perennial flower beds, the best time to clean them up is the spring. Leaving the long stalks over winter will keep snow present to insulate the plant roots from the cold and freeze-thaw cycles and add visual interest to your yard.

In the spring, put on some gloves and a long-sleeved shirt and head out to your beds! (My first day landscaping as a teenager was spent spring cleaning in a yard full of raspberries and rose bushes. I bore the scars on my arms for a long time!)

You can bend and break off the dried stalks of your perennial flowers or use a really large, sharp kitchen knife to slice off really thick ones. I leave the stalks a few inches or centimeters from the ground so I'm

Let Your Neighbors Know You're Organic!

Many environmental and health groups have lawn signs you can put up to let your neighbors know that your yard is Earth-friendly, organic, pesticide-free. Social marketers say that these signs help change the general ethos so that organic yard maintenance will become the acceptable norm. (Just think of how attitudes toward smoking have changed over the last decades.)

I've been told by many that in Halifax, Nova Scotia, where the regional authorities have not used pesticides since the late 1980s and a bylaw phasing out residential pesticide use came into effect in 2000, it is now socially unacceptable to spray anything on a yard. The parks manager told me they've stopped using organic tree sprays too. Why? They get so many public complaints from citizens who think the parks people are spraying chemicals.

Pesticide-free lawn sign

not risking pulling up the plant. Put the dried stalks in your compost bin, or you can lay them down to mulch your bed if you don't mind the look. I clear the leaves from the tops of low plants with my hands or with a light leaf rake. I leave most of the leaves around the plants to mulch the beds (see Chapter 7, Making Beds to Replace Your Lawn).

SUMMARY

• Refrain from using chemicals or potent organic solutions.
• Make sure your landscaping service is truly organic.
• Use natural mulches on your beds to retain moisture, prevent weeds and provide food to plants.
• Provide food to your plants naturally:
   – Use compost and actively aerated compost tea.
   – Leave grass clippings on your lawn.
   – Leave leaves on your beds or put them in your compost.
• Go for a more natural look to save labor, costs and non-renewable resources:
   – Accept some weeds.
   – Let grass grow long where it's a challenge to clip it.
   – Gradually replace your existing grass by overseeding with native grasses.
   – Replace lawn with shrubs, trees and flower beds.
• Use manual equipment as much as possible.

NOTES

1. The best soil biology lab tests are from the Soil Foodweb labs. Look up the nearest one to you at soilfoodweb.com.

2. Sara Williams, *Creating the Prairie Xeriscape: Low-maintenance, Water-efficient Gardening* (Saskatoon, SK: University Extension Press, University of Saskatchewan, 1997), 37.

3. The U.S.-based website beyondpesticides.org also has a page beyondpesticides.org/infoservices/pcos/TALKING.HTM of questions to ask your landscape service provider.

5

Weeds and Bugs

*Most insect visitors should inspire you with a sense of
wonder... only a very few wreak havoc in the garden.*
— Nora Bryan and Ruth Staal

Fungal strands

**Are you ready to be a Gardener? Working with weeds and
bugs can be your best opportunity to learn to work in
harmony with nature, rather than trying to combat and
control. That old Warrior way ends up being a losing battle
for just about every being in your eco-yard. The winners may
be the weeds and bugs that come in after the battle. Soil
microbes and organic matter now depleted, conditions are
prime for colonization—ideal for weeds! And the bugs and
birds that prey on nasty insects? Gone!**

The good news is that the Gardener approach to working with weeds
and bugs is usually a lot less work—a "live and let live approach" is
often best. The basic premise is to design your eco-yard to work as a
natural ecosystem and then work with nature to support it.

I. Addressing Weeds—Nature's First Responders!

Weeds can be easier to accept if you appreciate them for the critical
role they play in the ecosystem. Weeds are nature's first responders.

When land is disturbed (e.g., dug up, or after a landslide), weeds come in to colonize the bare soil. They prevent soil erosion and prepare the way for other plants to grow. Weeds are also able to grow where other plants cannot grow very well because the soil is poor in certain nutrients or lacking the soil microbes to make nutrients available to plants. Many weeds bring minerals up to the surface from deep in the soil through their long roots. When they die and decay, they release those minerals back into the soil in a form available to other plants; weeds act to heal the soil.[1]

Many weeds have specific uses in herbal medicine for healing too. In fact, the origin of the word "weed" is from the Anglo-Saxon *weod* or "little herb."[2] An herbalist once told me with a smile that on her farm she cultivates plots of "weeds" other people try to eliminate.

PLANT ALL BARE AREAS OR COVER WITH MULCH

Weeds will be the first plants to grow in any bare soil areas. Covering all your bare soil with plants will prevent weeds. Groundcover plants that spread over a wide area are good for this. Other bare areas should be covered with an organic mulch, such as wood chips or leaves, to a depth of 4 to 6 in. (10 to 15 cm). (See Chapter 7, Making Beds to Replace Your Lawn for more details.) The mulch will prevent weed seeds in the soil from germinating. Neither of these methods will completely prevent weeds, but both will greatly reduce them.

MINIMIZE GRASS

Weeds in lawns are the most difficult to deal with. So minimizing lawn area will reduce your maintenance work and costs. Limit grass to those areas where children or pets play or where you want a picnic site. Where you don't need grass, you can plant trees, shrubs and perennial flowers (flowers that bloom every year) that grow well in your area. Cover the open areas around the plants with natural mulch (wood chips are usually best) to prevent weeds. You could also have decks, patios, waterfalls and other features instead of lawn.

**Those Roots May Be Long,
but It Doesn't Mean They're Strong**

Weeds put most of their energy into quick growth and seeding in order to spread quickly. Only 20 percent of the energy most weeds produce by photosynthesis goes to the roots vs. 60 percent in grasses and 80 percent in trees and shrubs.[3] Given that most weeds have less-developed root systems, other plants can out-compete weeds for water and nutrients if the soil is healthy.

LET YOUR WEEDS TELL YOU WHAT'S NEEDED FOR HEALTH

When weeds really flourish in an area, it may be that the area has been recently disturbed or that the soil ecosystem is out of balance. Spreading compost and actively aerated compost tea will help rebalance your soil. Wood chip mulch on your beds or even really small wood chips on your lawn will also help rebuild fungi in the soil. Fungi hold calcium in the soil and also make it available to plants. Weeds tend to flourish where other plants can't get enough calcium. Some experts say that adding calcium to your yard will rebalance the minerals more quickly than compost alone. See Amending Soil Chemistry in Chapter 8 for more on how to do this.

ACCEPT AND BENEFIT FROM HAVING SOME WEEDS

Accept and benefit from having some weeds. For example, dandelions, with their deep tap roots, are great soil aerators. You can use young dandelion leaves in salads, or make dandelion wine. This is what the French do! A tonic made from dandelion roots is cleansing for your liver and will help it clear out toxins (such as pesticides!). Dandelion flowers are some of the first to bloom in the spring. They support beneficial insects such as bees and butterflies during that time when few other flowers are blooming.

Lamb's quarters, also known as pigweed or goosefoot, is a weed that has an upright form with lovely green leaves, sometimes with a reddish

Making Dandelion Tonic

Use organic dandelions (chemical herbicides or fertilizers have not been applied on or near them for at least two years). Dig out the tap roots, rinse them and chop them into pieces ½ in. (1 cm) long. Bring to a boil and then simmer for 10 minutes. I make a big pot of dandelion tonic in the spring and store it in a juice jar in the fridge. Several times a day I'll add a few ounces (40 mL) to a glass of water or juice and drink it until it's gone. It tastes bitter and I like that—a bit of honey makes it smoother going down.

tinge. Lamb's quarters is very nutritious and tastes a lot like spinach. In one yard where I lived, I let the lamb's quarters grow in my flowerbeds and picked the leaves to steam with my morning eggs and salsa.[4] Once I'd harvested the leaves, I would pull out the plants, pick off any seed heads to put in the garbage, and then throw the remainder in my compost bin.

If you let your weeds go to seed (flower and then produce seeds which spread), you will have more weeds. Make regular weeding part of your routine (every few weeks) to keep them in check. Do the weeding just after weeds flower and before they go to seed. This will allow insects to benefit from the flowers and still prevent weed spread.

A yard with some dandelions and weeds is a great sign that the steward is refraining from using chemicals in that yard. I look for weeds in public places to know where a healthy place will be for me to sit on the lawn or on benches. Friends of mine from Europe tell me that dandelions are no big deal there. It seems pretty strange to them that many North Americans devote so much energy to getting rid of

Weeding as Self-care

I have friends who use weeding as their meditation time. A young working mom told me that working in her garden (usually weeding!) for half an hour is worth a few hours of yoga or meditation. Weeding is her preferred way to rejuvenate.

Weeding tree-root suckers

dandelions. Personally I love the look of dandelions in bloom. In one of my yards, I would simply go out and pick off the seed heads once they turned fluffy so they wouldn't blow into the neighbors' yards.

SPREAD CORN GLUTEN ON YOUR YARD TO PREVENT WEEDS

Processed from corn, corn gluten meal comes in the form of small granules that you can spread over your yard with a hand-held spreader or a fertilizer spreader. Corn gluten prevents weed seeds from sprouting and is most useful when applied in the spring before weed seeds germinate. You can also apply it in the fall for some effect in the spring. Corn gluten is usually available in the spring and fall at garden centers and organic grocery stores. If you have extra (often a bag will be enough for two applications), store it in a sealed container so that mice can't get at it.

According to Jim Ross of the Prairie Turfgrass Research Center at Olds College in Olds, Alberta, corn gluten works well to prevent new weeds if the weeds that are already there are eradicated. (This means digging them out!) Ross says 96 percent of new dandelions come from the spring seeds that disperse. Those seeds sprout within two to three weeks, so if corn gluten is applied around then, it is most helpful.

Corn gluten prevents weed germination   Spreading corn gluten

Corn gluten also acts as a mild fertilizer and will stimulate the growth of your grass, which may require more mowing.[5]

Corn Gluten: A Caution

Caution: Do not use corn gluten on areas where you are overseeding new grass on your lawn, or are planting other seeds. It will prevent your seeds from sprouting. You can spread corn gluten about a month after your seeds have sprouted.

REMOVE WEEDS BY DIGGING

Many weeds can simply be pulled out by hand, especially when the ground is moist. All digging and drilling tools work best when the ground is moist, so it is best to weed within a day or two after a rainfall or after watering.

Dispose of Weed Seeds in Trash, Not Compost

It is best to throw weed seeds out in the garbage (trash) rather than in your compost, unless you know that your compost will heat to at least 150°F (66°C), hot enough to destroy the seeds.

Dandelions and thistles have deep tap roots (a tap root grows straight down into the soil). These roots usually need to be dug out of the ground to at least 4 in. (10 cm) deep, or the plant will grow back.

Hand digging tools

Hand digging tools have a handle and a long metal prong (usually the longer the better) with a fork at the end. Just push in beside the root, lever the prong back and forth to make a hole around the root and then pull or pry the root out.

Step digging tools

Step digging tools, which tend to be easy on the back, generally work well if the ground is moist. Standing upright, you step on the pedal to push the prongs in around the root. Then you twist a few times in one direction and pull out a plug of soil with the root. If the ground is dry, you will only pull out about 2 in. (5 cm) of root—usually not enough to stop it from growing back. When the ground is moist, enough of the root comes out to be effective.

Using step digging tools for weeding lawn
1. *Step down*   **2**. *Twist and pull*   **3**. *Push out weed into compost pail*

Another sturdy type of step digging tool features a slanted piece of metal under the step plate. You step to push the slanted piece vertically down beside the weed and then pull the handle sideways to loosen the weed and pull it out. This tool works really well in beds, but I found it chewed up the lawn more than other step digging tools. Perhaps I wasn't well enough practiced with it—the process certainly provided some aeration for the lawn!

Using a slant step digger to weed a bed **1**. *Step* **2**. *Lever and pull weed*

Drill-attached weeder

Another popular weeding tool consists of a long metal pole with a small blade at the bottom. The pole attaches to a portable drill. You drill down as deep as you can into the root. The blade chews up the root so that it won't grow back. If you use a battery-operated drill, you need a model with at least 18 volts of power. If the weeds are growing around tree roots, especially around poplars, you may not be able to get enough of the root out with this tool to be effective in preventing the weeds from growing back.

Water pressure weeder

This tool attaches to your hose. You push it down into the ground near the root of the weed, and the water pressure loosens the root so you can pull it out. When I used it, I found that the nozzle tended to plug up, and I still had to find a way to pull out the root. Yet I know that others love this tool.

Blade tool for weeding cracks

Weeds that are growing in cracks, for example, between concrete blocks, can be dug out with a knife. Some specialty garden stores or tools stores (e.g., Lee Valley Tools) sell a curved blade fixed to a handle. You hook the blade around the weed roots to pull them out.

Horticultural vinegar or boiling water for weeds in sidewalk cracks

Horticultural vinegar, available at garden centers, is often not called "horticultural vinegar"; rather, look on the label for "acetic acid." This strong vinegar solution works well for weeds that are established. For weeds in the early stage of growth, the less potent household vinegar, with a little lemon juice, will do fine. Use gloves. If you spray vinegar, or pour boiling water, it will harm all the plants it touches and kill the soil microbes too, so use these methods in sidewalk cracks or away from other desired plants. It usually takes a few applications over time to kill the weeds.

If you really want a healthy eco-yard, it's best to think health and prevention for your soil and plants and some exercise for you; refrain from using potent substances such as horticultural vinegar! Tree roots, fungi and microbes can grow even under sidewalk blocks. Let them flourish there.

II. Loving Bugs—The Workhorses of Your Eco-yard

Come to know and love the amazing role insects play in your eco-yard. They help your plants reproduce through pollination, they break down plant litter to create soil, they keep other insects in check, they provide food for birds, fish and small animals—and they're beautiful! Rather

Hats Off to the Average Working Bug

By turning and aerating the soil, ants are second only to earthworms in improving its texture. Earthworms build tunnels for water and nutrients to move through. Even large worms that bring clay lumps to the surface provide benefit to the soil, as well as reflexology for your bare feet! Bees and butterflies pollinate your plants. So do wasps and flies! They also prey on other insects such as caterpillars. And many caterpillars turn into butterflies. Beetles such as ladybugs prey on other insects, such as aphids. Spiders are especially important predators.

Ants   Earthworm in soil

than try to control insects, you can work with them to build a healthy ecosystem in your yard.

DESIGN FOR INSECTS

Diversity of plants leads to diversity of insects

Plant a wide variety of plants in your yard. Insects that eat or infest plants usually just go for one species, so if one type of plant gets eaten, you will still have many other types. A diversity of plants will attract a diversity of insects to pollinate your plants and prey on each other to keep all insect species in balance. Nectar-bearing flowering plants will attract important predators such as wasps and hoverflies. Design so that you have flowers all season long to support predators and pollinators, especially early in the season when few flowers bloom. Native plant species will provide more support to native pollinators and the local native ecosystem.

Spread similar plants around your yard

Spread similar plants around your yard. For example, rather than having all your currant bushes or lettuce in one spot, scatter them around your yard. That way, if one plant becomes a host for a "problem" insect or disease, you can address the problem before it damages all of those plants.

Healthy plants aren't bothered by insects

Insects go for the easy meal and will chew on plants that are weak. Choose hardy plants suited to the ecosystem of your yard (see

Chapter 10, Designing Your Eco-yard). Plants thrive and stay healthy when conditions are right for them (e.g., appropriate moisture levels, sunshine, soil type). Keep your plants healthy by spreading compost on your soil and spraying actively aerated compost tea on your plants.

Avoid plants that tend to attract problem insects

Some plants attract insects every year. For example, Virginia creeper vines often attract leafhoppers, which chew up the leaves and drop off the vines onto people sitting or walking below; leafhoppers are often considered a nuisance. Plant other vines instead, such as honeysuckle or clematis.

ACCEPT SOME INSECT OR DISEASE ACTIVITY

Insects need to eat. If their munching doesn't hurt your plants too much or look too bad, then accept it! Often insects have periodic cycles and will only be abundant once every few years. Some of those munching caterpillars may turn into butterflies—great pollinators. Ladybug larvae may look like something to be wary of (black with reddish spots), yet they will develop into beetles that eat aphids.

Insects such as aphids reproduce so fast that you won't be able to control them, even with pesticides. They rarely harm plants, so let the predators, like ladybugs, eat them!

So-called plant diseases are often caused by pathogenic, or harmful, bacteria or fungi. Unlike the soil microbes that are the foundation for healthy plants and soil, these feed off plants in ways unhealthy to the plant. Some plants are just prone to attracting certain pathogens. For example, many plants get powdery mildew—a whitish powdery substance on their leaves caused by fungi.

Watering the soil around these plants, rather than the leaves, helps prevent powdery mildew. Plants prone to powdery mildew, such as *Centaurea montana* (perennial cornflower), tend to get it more after they flower, so if the look of the leaves bothers me, I just cut the plant back and dispose of the foliage.

WHEN YOU FEEL YOU NEED TO ACT

If the insects or diseases are damaging your yard to a level unacceptable to you, you can try some methods that generally are healthy for the ecosystem of your yard. First, make sure there really is a problem. Look at a book that will help you identify garden insects. Guides are available for various regions (e.g., prairie and Alberta books are listed in Resources, near the end of the book). Alternatively you could take a photo of the bug or plant, or a leaf or twig sample, to a local garden center. Most large garden centers have staff members who can help you identify insect and disease problems and advise you on how to address them. Ask them for non-toxic ways to do so!

Hose them off!

Using a spray nozzle capable of a powerful burst, you can spray "pest" insects, such as aphids or leafhoppers, off plant leaves. You may need to repeat this every few days during the height of their activity. As a preventive measure during hot, dry spells, you can spray plants prone to spider mites every few days, since spider mites thrive in hot, dry conditions.

Spray them with soap

You can purchase insecticidal soap at stores that sell gardening supplies. You can also make your own soap spray by mixing one tablespoon (15 mL) of dishwashing liquid in two quarts (2 L) of warm water. Spray it on the plants from a hand spray bottle. Soap kills insects on contact, so spray wherever there are insects—look on *and* under the leaves. After spraying, rinse the soap off the plants with lots of water to prevent coating the leaves and harming the plant.

Soap spray will work against aphids, earwigs, mealy bugs, mites, sawfly larvae and white flies. Beneficial insects are said not to be affected by soap spray, but I wouldn't deliberately spray them!

Soap spray should be used with caution as it can harm your plants. It poses a low risk to birds and mammals but a high risk to fish.[6]

Pick and prune

You can pick and squish insects or drown them in a bucket of water. Or you could throw them where birds can find and eat them (e.g., driveway, roof). Make it a fun family activity—kids of any age will likely want to help! Prune off leaves and branches affected by insects or disease and place them in the trash, not your compost; you don't want the problem to spread to other plants.

To manage insects that attack trees from within, such as elm bark beetles, prune affected branches and place them in the trash. With any plant you have identified as diseased, consider removing it and trashing it before the disease spreads. It is easier to prevent spread than to address widespread disease.

Pruning Is More Than Just a Haircut!

Proper pruning is important. If you need to prune, you may want to look online or obtain one of the many good books on pruning. Here are some guidelines:

• Use clean, sharp equipment.

• If you are pruning diseased plants, clean your blades with diluted bleach (10 parts water to 1 part bleach) or hydrogen peroxide between cuts.

• Cut large branches off in sections from the end, so that the weight of the branch does not tear it off.

• For larger branches, cut outside the branch collar (a little swelling where the branch emerges).

• Cut perpendicular to the branch you are pruning and make a clean cut.

• Avoid using pruning spray or tar. Let the cut heal naturally.

PUT UP BARRIERS

Slugs crawl around on a big foot. Because they need water, they usually eat plants growing in moist conditions, often in the shade (hostas, for instance). Slugs shred plant leaves, leave a shiny trail of slime and are most active in the middle of the night. But they can be kept away from your plants with all kinds of creative barriers. Slugs don't like metal, so

Slug-picking at Dawn

Early morning slug-picking is one way to commune with your moist garden areas. Boards placed near your slug-eaten plants will collect slugs on the moist underside. Lift the board to pick the slugs off. Half grapefruit shells or orange peels can be placed as slug tents for them to collect. You can then dispose of the slug-laden fruit peels. Bowls with beer garner mixed reviews in terms of effectiveness.

copper tape or foil can be shaped around slug-prone plants or container edges. You can find copper at garden suppliers and stained glass supply outlets. Other barriers for slugs include anything they would not want to crawl across—sand or sharp gravel, hair clippings, broken egg shells. These barriers need to be freshened up regularly.

Diatomaceous Earth

Diatomaceous earth (DE) is a commercial product used in filtering water for hydroponic growing systems. Made up of ancient seashells, it comes in gravel and powder form. DE has gained some currency amongst gardeners as a way to kill crawling insects. Many writers claim that the hard edges in the tiny diatom crystals scratch the insect bodies and they die. However, an entomologist and former teacher of mine informed me that "scratch and die" is not actually how DE works. Through microscopes, we watched as soil microbes cruised over diatoms happily. Rather, he explained, DE contains a lot of chitin, the same material that makes up the shells of many insects (e.g., ants, beetles). When DE is sprinkled in your garden, the soil microbes that eat chitin multiply. Insects sense this and go elsewhere to avoid having their shells eaten by microbes.[7]

I use DE gravel on top of the soil in my houseplants to deter aphids. It works pretty well—we still sometimes have aphids. I have also used DE gravel around wooden yard features that were being eaten by carpenter ants. It did seem to chase away some of the ants. But I'm leery now of using DE in my eco-yard because I don't want to chase away the beneficial insects.

Collars made from plastic flower pots or bottles can protect seedlings or tender plants. Usually these are used on vegetables such as cabbages against cutworms. Place the collar in the soil about 1 in. (3 cm) deep around the plant.

Row covers—breathable cloths that allow water and air but not bugs in—can be placed over rows of vegetables or even over individual plants.

Bring in predators

You can also control problem insects with other insects or microbes. Use these with care, though; you don't want to introduce a non-native species that will become invasive. For example, there is some thought that the ladybugs sold at garden centers or online may displace more effective native ladybugs.

"Biological controls" in general should be used discreetly to prevent resistance. Commercial greenhouses, for example, sometimes use specific bacteria to control specific pests. Sometimes the pests become resistant to the bacteria, so it's advisable to use this type of thing only when really necessary. And who's to say flying insect predators, such as aphids or praying mantis, will even stay in your yard once you release them? Your solution may be (very) short-term. I suggest using imported predators only when you have a real problem.

SUMMARY

- You can prevent most weed and bug problems through designing your yard as a natural ecosystem and working with nature to support it; try to introduce diversity and use plants suited to the conditions.
- Keep your eco-yard healthy with compost and actively aerated compost tea—weeds and bugs will stay away.
- Take a "live and let live" approach.
- If you need to act, use non-toxic methods.
- Let your weeds and bugs teach you how to be a Gardener.

NOTES

1. Jay L. McCaman, *Weeds and Why They Grow* (Sand Lake, MI: Jay L. McCaman, 1994).

2. See Note 1.

3. My class notes for Introduction to Soil Biology course taught by Matthew George, Soil Foodweb Canada Ltd., Vulcan, AB, September 24–25, 2007.

4. Herbalist Terry Willard recommends eating lamb's quarters in moderation.

5. Jim Ross, Olds College, Prairie Turfgrass Research Institute, personal communication, March 28, 2007.

6. Québec, Ministère du Développement durable, de l'Environnement et des Parcs, "Relative toxicity of the main active ingredients contained in pesticides for domestic use used for green spaces" (September 2008), mddep.gouv.qc.ca/pesticides/jardiner-en/toxicite.pdf.

7. Joe Whaley (class presentation, Soil Foodweb Management Training Program, Soil Foodweb Canada Ltd., Vulcan, AB, March 24, 2007). Joe Whaley is an entomologist and former Executive Director of the Sustainable Studies Institute in Corvallis, OR.

6

What's in a Lawn?

No occupation is so delightful to me as the culture of the Earth, and no culture comparable to that of the garden. —Thomas Jefferson

Flagellates

A few years ago a couple from the Philippines asked me to help them with their Calgary front yard—an expanse of dry grass and dandelions. "We don't know how to look after lawn—in Philippines everyone had fruit trees and flowers in their yards!" I supervised a volunteer work crew of friends and family that replaced their lawn with a beautiful rock patio and pathway wandering through flowers, trees and shrubs in beds mulched with wood chips. After 12 years in their suburb, the couple began to meet their neighbors, who came to admire their flowers and landscaping.

From Lawn to Fruit and Flowers

Our front yard has become a conversation piece. Our neighbors come to ask about our plants and tell us they appreciate what we've done. Our yard has also increased environmental awareness among our friends and family. For example, our children and parents now understand that wood chips keep in moisture and add organic matter to the soil. As we walk through parks or visit gardens around the city, we can now identify perennial plants, native flowers and trees that we used to overlook. – Cesar Cala and Marichu Antonio. (See the color pages for photos.)

In most countries, yards have little if any lawn. So how did we come to have such an unsustainable lawn-dominated landscape in North America? Fashion and marketing!

I. A Short History of the North American Lawn

Lawns began as a way to protect castles in medieval Europe.[1] Grassed areas around castles were kept short so that attackers could be seen. The grass was cut by serfs with scythes or cropped by grazing animals.

CASTLE PROTECTION BECOMES STATUS SYMBOL

Formal gardens with clipped lawns became fashionable among the aristocracy first in 17th-century France and then in England. In the 18th century, some English landscape designers went further, cutting trees and levelling large areas of land on country estates to create vast expanses of grass. Only the wealthy could afford to build these lawns and hire the labour to maintain them by hand.

The influence of a few urban planners and landscape designers in the late 1800s made the high-maintenance lawn a desirable status symbol for the middle class too.

LAWNS COME TO NORTH AMERICA

Wealthy North Americans, like Thomas Jefferson, brought this fashion of leveled turf areas to their estates, even though North American conditions are not as favourable as in England for grass. Jefferson, like many other wealthy Americans, had slaves to tend his lawn.

Urban planning in North America started to involve larger front yards for city houses and common areas for lawn sports like croquet and tennis. The lawn came to be viewed as the center of family recreation. The invention of the lawn mower in the late 1800s enabled more people to maintain a lawn. Grass varieties were imported from overseas as local varieties had been depleted by overgrazing—what became Bermuda grass came from Africa, and what is now known as Kentucky bluegrass from Europe and North Asia.

KENTUCKY BLUEGRASS LAWNS— TREND BECOMES CONVENTION

Then in the 1870s, Frederick Olmsted, the influential landscape architect who designed Mount Royal Park in Montreal and Central Park in New York, wrote that the ideal, in planning suburbs, was open expanses of lawn. Other designers followed suit, and lawns became the convention.

In the early 1900s, garden clubs began forming to promote well-maintained gardens and lawns. The post-war boom of the 1950s, along with the expansion of the suburbs, the invention of the power mower and the growth of home and garden magazines, meant the situation was ripe for marketers to promote their pesticides, fertilizers, mowers and other tools as necessary to keep up with the neighbors' well-trimmed green lawn. Lawn was now the convention for North American landscaping, even in areas of western North America such as the eastern slopes of the Rockies and the Great Plains where conditions aren't suitable for the typical grasses used in these lawns (mostly Kentucky bluegrass), necessitating lots of added water and nutrition.

New Markets for Nerve Gas

Chemical pesticides were first used in the Second World War as nerve gases for chemical warfare! They had the side effect of killing tree leaves. After the war, chemical companies found whole new applications for these chemicals in agriculture, forestry and landscape maintenance as fungicides, insecticides and herbicides.[2]

KENTUCKY BLUEGRASS LAWN IS NOT ENVIRONMENTALLY SUSTAINABLE

Large expanses of mowed blue-green turf grass are costly to maintain in most locales in North America. This is because Kentucky bluegrass—the standard grass variety used in sod and most seed mixes sold in North America—does not grow well in hot, dry conditions. It also naturally turns brown in dry climates after its spring growing spurt. So most of our current lawns and many urban green spaces need lots of water and fertilizer to look green or "attractive." Then, once watered and fed, they need mowing. (In fact, any lawn usually takes more work to maintain than a flower, shrub and tree bed or a deck or patio. Depending on where you live, your lawn may look dry and brown for much of the year too, no matter what type of grass you use.)

Water-greedy lawn

istockphoto.com/Sally Scott

And because Kentucky bluegrass doesn't grow that well in most climates, it's more likely weeds will take up residence. To deal with the weeds, people tend to use chemical pesticides, which in turn kill microorganisms in the soil (see Chapter 8, Soil: A Feeding Frenzy), making the grass even less healthy and prompting the use of more fertilizer and water. This cycle is not environmentally sustainable in the long term.

This is why the best way to go for an attractive, low-maintenance eco-yard is to minimize the amount of lawn you have to just the area your family will use for play or picnics or lying on the grass. And replace the grass in any lawn you have with a type suited to your climate.

Kentucky Bluegrass Voted Most Noxious Weed in Canada in CBC Poll

For a week in August 2007, the CBC Radio program *Sounds Like Canada* asked listeners to send in their vote for the worst weed in Canada. Kentucky bluegrass won! Six other so-called noxious weeds, such as Canada thistle, were in the running.

WATER-WISE LANDSCAPING IS THE WAY OF THE FUTURE

Water-wise landscapes, including hardy grasses that need little water, are best for eco-yards.

During the droughts of the 1970s, a xeriscape movement began in the western United States. Xeriscapes are landscapes that need little water—mainly by the use of local (native) and drought-tolerant species of grass and plants. Xeriscaping, also called water-wise gardening, does not necessarily mean a garden full of cactus! A wide variety of lush-looking plants work well.

In 1981, the Colorado government, universities and the landscape industry came up with steps everyone could take to reduce the effects of future droughts there, including xeriscaping. By 1990, programs were in place in many areas of North America, often with the municipal water supplier as a key partner.

Many towns and cities have been successful in promoting water conservation methods so their water use doesn't exceed their supply. Fast growth rates in cities like Calgary and current trends in climate change make it likely that water use for yards will be restricted in the future. (Calgary's municipal government has already instituted a Water Wise program in the city.)

Landscape use generally takes 40 to 70 percent of the treated water supply, and half of this watering is either wasted or not needed.[3] Spending money on water treatment and distribution facilities for water-greedy landscaping is not an effective use of taxpayer dollars.

The late 20th-century blue-green Kentucky bluegrass standard lawn is being replaced by a new assortment of landscapes that are friendlier to the environment and our wallets. Grasses used are more adapted to the local climate. Some people are growing native flowers in their lawn and using low groundcovers instead of grass. Variety is increasingly welcomed with creative features such as front yard vegetable gardens, meadows, aspen groves, outdoor kitchens and mixed tree, shrub and flower beds.

II. Eco-lawns

An eco-lawn is a lawn that takes little watering or tending. It is usually made up of native or hardy grasses suited to the local ecosystem and conditions of the yard. Many of these grasses grow short and slowly so they need little if any mowing. Other low-water-use plants can be grown in an eco-lawn too—such as clover or chamomile.

Below are instructions for slowly transforming your current lawn to an eco-lawn by overseeding, including information on types of grasses you can use and how to seed a new lawn.

OVERSEEDING

Overseeding is adding new grass seed to your existing lawn so it grows more thickly. Weeds are less likely to grow where the grass is hardy and thick. Overseeding is one way to replace the grass types you have with those that are more suited to the conditions in your yard or need less water.

When to overseed

Overseeding is most effective when done in the spring or fall, when the weather is not hot and the tender grass seedlings will do well. In Calgary, for example, May, June and September are good months to overseed. You will have to water daily for about ten minutes (when it doesn't rain) to keep the seedlings moist so they will sprout. For those in snowy climes, overseeding in late fall is easiest. You need not water at all—just let the winter snow melt and spring rain encourage the seeds to sprout in the spring. You won't get quite as many seeds germinating with this method, however; it may be an extra year before the overseeding really takes.

Avoid using corn gluten meal, a natural weed suppressant, for a month before and after overseeding or it will stop the seeds from sprouting.

Two to four years for new grass types to take over

Generally you need to overseed once a year for two to four years for the hardier grass types to take over your lawn. Your grass will be thicker and greener during the process. If you want the hardy grass types to establish themselves sooner, stop watering your lawn once the new seeds have sprouted and are a couple of inches or centimeters high. The hardier grasses will then compete better with the grasses currently in your lawn (e.g., Kentucky bluegrass). If you're in a hurry, you could overseed in the spring and then again in the early fall.

Spread a thin layer of compost to overseed

Spreading compost on a lawn with the back of a rake

Spread a ½ in. or 1 cm layer of compost over your lawn first so that the grass seed has something to sprout in. (See Using the Humus, in Chapter 9, The Wonders of Compost, for specific instructions.)

Then use a seeder to spread the grass seed. A drop seeder will spread the seeds more accurately than a broadcast seeder. Spread half the seed you need in one direction back and forth over your lawn. Then spread the other half of your seed over your lawn by going back

Seeding grass with a drop seeder

Raking grass seed to cover with compost

and forth in the other direction. Use the amount of grass seed recommended by the seed supplier or on the bag. This is usually about 5 pounds (2 kilograms) of grass seed for 1,000 square feet (95 square meters) of lawn area. Rake the seed into the compost lightly with a leaf rake so the seed is covered.

Landscaping contractors are available to overseed your lawn for you. For large areas, a blower truck is often used to spray the seed and the compost over your lawn at the same time.

Use a slit seeder to overseed

Landscapers may also use a slit seeder—a power machine that cuts a small slit into your lawn and drops grass seeds into that slit. With a slit seeder, spreading compost is not necessary, although it's still great for your lawn to spread compost over top. You may be able to rent a slit seeder if for some reason spreading compost is not your best option.

Refrain From Roundup!

Some grass seed suppliers suggest that you apply Roundup to your current lawn to kill it so you can overseed new grass. Refrain from doing this! Roundup and other products in which glyphosate is the main ingredient are said to be biodegradable. This may be so, but biodegradability does not mean it's a benign product! Glyphosate formulations have been found to cause DNA abnormalities that can lead to cancer and also to cause genetic mutations.[4] They have also been found to interfere with enzymes involved with hormone production in mice[5] and hormone function in human placenta cells.[6] Roundup can get into a plant's circulatory system through the roots and harm it. An arborist has told me she has seen many problems in nearby trees when homeowners have used Roundup on the weeds in their lawn and sidewalks.

When I first learned about Roundup many years ago, I was thrilled that here was an easy way to kill weeds my neighbors may not want to see in my yard. (Yes—I have changed over my years of gardening!) I happily sprayed the dandelions and grass in the cracks of my sidewalk and against my house, and it worked! The weeds turned brown and died in a few days. A less naïve friend suggested that such a potent substance probably had some effects on other life. My enthusiasm tempered, I stopped using Roundup.

Now I realize that anything that kills is probably going to harm other living beings. I feel it's better to forgo the killers and focus on building and restoring natural health and life in the soil and plants. And I like the look of things growing in sidewalk cracks! As a landscaper, I now plant beautiful plants in such crevices.

A NEW TREND IN GRASSES

The new trend in the grass seed industry, as consumers demand it, is for grasses that require little water or fertilizer and that grow slowly or short, requiring little mowing.

Following are some alternatives to the standard Kentucky bluegrass—a blue-green grass that spreads by its roots.

Sheep's fescue

Sheep's fescue

Sheep's fescue grass is found in many varieties across North America, Europe and Asia. Seed suppliers sell a dark green, fine-leaved type that grows in little bunches and spreads by seed. Sheep's fescue works well for a lawn. It is especially suited to shade and will grow in dry shade. I've had success with growing it under overhangs of houses where rain does not fall. Once established, sheep's fescue is even and soft to the touch.

Sheep's fescue grass boasts several advantages:

- It will not invade flower and shrub beds, as it does not spread by its roots.
- Where I live in Calgary, it only grows 6 to 8 in. (15 to 20 centimeters) high, then lies down in swirls for a nice effect. It can be left unmowed.
- It grows slowly and needs mowing (if you mow) once a month at most.
- Once it greens up in the spring, it stays green most of the season without watering.
- It grows densely and out-competes weeds.
- It grows well in sun and shade.

Some say sheep's fescue will not do as well in heavy-traffic areas (where it is regularly walked on). At Bow Point Nursery near Calgary, sheep's fescue has been growing since 2005 on a road that is driven over fairly regularly by trucks. The grass is holding up well.

Hard and creeping fescues

Other varieties of fescue grasses also work well for eco-lawns. Like sheep's fescue, they are bunch grasses that grow in little clumps. Some of these grow a little taller than the sheep's fescue and may require more mowing. Some of the hard fescues, like Rocky Mountain fescue, are more suited than sheep's fescue to really hot, sunny areas.

Creeping fescues will creep and spread. But these varieties are still not nearly as invasive in neighboring flowerbeds as Kentucky bluegrass.

Blue grama grass

Blue grama is a short grass native to the prairies and very drought tolerant. Its leaves grow in tufts, and its seed heads look like eyebrows on a short stalk.

Grass trials

In the mid-1990s, the Prairie Turfgrass Research Center at Olds College, near Calgary, performed trials in southern and central Alberta on low-maintenance grasses. They seeded areas with various grasses and grass mixes and watched them for a few years. The results showed that the hard, creeping and sheep's fescues and also the blue grama grass did pretty well in terms of establishing and covering the area, competing with weeds and tolerating dry conditions.

Perennial ryegrass, a common seed in many grass mixes, did not show as much tolerance for dry conditions. Many of the grasses native to Alberta took too long to establish and had a lot of weeds.

What grass type to use

For the Prairie provinces and Northern Great Plains states in North America, I recommend overseeding or seeding bare soil with straight sheep's fescue grass in areas that are not sun-baked. In really sunny areas, I recommend a low-maintenance mix. Seed suppliers sell different mixes; I'm still learning which to use in specific conditions. The company Brett-Young uses two kinds of hard fescue and Reuben's Canada bluegrass in their low-maintenance mix. Jim Ross of Olds College recommends a mix of sheep's fescue, Rocky Mountain fescue and creeping red fescue. A mix of this kind can be helpful as it covers all the bases; in varying conditions through the years, one type or the other will grow better. In future editions of *Eco-yards*, I may have more information on low-maintenance grasses for different regions of the

Grass Seed Mix-Up

The usual reason for using a mix of grass seeds is that faster-growing grasses shade and protect the slower growing grasses. While almost all books recommend planting mixtures, it's not necessary, especially if you are overseeding existing grass. My experience with overseeding and planting straight sheep's fescue grass is that it establishes itself well, by itself.

world. Ask your local seed suppliers to recommend a low-maintenance grass type. (You may have to stress you want an alternative to Kentucky bluegrass.)

Seeding a new lawn

Sod that you can buy in rolls to plant over prepared soil is all Kentucky bluegrass-based. Fescues and other hardy grasses generally root too deeply to be grown as commercial sod. So, if you are starting your lawn from scratch, or want to start your lawn over, your best bet is to seed on prepared soil.

The best thing you can do for your lawn is to have 8 in. (20 cm) of great soil, rich with organic matter, beneath it. Your lawn will grow better, resist weeds better and need less water in the long run. Most topsoil available for purchase is full of weed seeds because it has been piled up somewhere and the weed seeds have spread. This topsoil is also usually not very rich in organic life. If you are looking for great soil, ask your supplier where the topsoil comes from and how it has been handled—if it has all been composted to higher than 150°F (66°C), then it could be fine. For example, Bow Point Nursery near Calgary has composted weed-free soil available in bulk (see contact information in the Resources section at the end of the book). You can also bring in really good compost and rototill it in with your topsoil.

Rake your soil out flat and apply the grass seed with a drop seeder (seed will spread more evenly than with a broadcast seeder—the whirly kind). For the most even seed coverage, spread half of the seed while moving back and forth in one direction and the other half moving in a perpendicular direction.

What If My Soil Does Have Weed Seeds?

Don't sweat! Those weeds will sprout fast and provide a great service of shading and protecting your grass seedlings as they sprout and grow. Those weeds will also be shallow-rooted and easy to pull once your grass seedlings have established themselves and no longer need the protection. My parents, as young homeowners, brought in new soil, rototilled it into their yard and seeded their lawn before going away on a two-week vacation. They were aghast on coming home to a yard full of foot-high stinkweed in bloom, shining white in their headlights. Later, though, they were relieved to find the soil moist due to the stinkweed cover; the grass had started growing nicely. They just had to spend a few hours pulling all the weeds.

Seed sources

Your local garden centers or nurseries probably don't have fescue-based grass seed mixes. If you buy at these places, look for grass mixes that will have the lowest percentage of Kentucky bluegrass.

Seed suppliers can make you custom grass seed mixes or sell you just one type of seed. You usually have to order custom mixes in large quantities, but give your local seed supplier a call and ask if they will sell you just enough to plant or overseed your lawn. Or share with your neighbors. Generally you will need 5 pounds (2 kilograms) of grass seed for 1,000 square feet or 95 square meters of lawn area. Ask your local seed supplier what they would recommend for your area in the way of really hardy grasses that don't need much water or fertilizer. (For a recommended Alberta supplier, see the Resources section at the end of the book.)

III. New Lawn or Old: Making the Best of a Bad Lot

KEEP YOUR LAWN LUSH AND HEALTHY

In the long run, keeping grass only where you really use it is a lower-maintenance option and generally best for the environment. Most yards have lawn, however, and you may not yet have gotten around to replacing it. So here are some natural landscaping practices for a healthy, lush lawn.

Overseed

Overseeding is the practice of adding new grass seed to your lawn so it grows more thickly. Overseeding can be used to replace the grass type in your lawn with a more hardy type that needs less water—and it helps prevent weeds. (See the first part of this chapter for details on how to overseed.)

Mow high

If you set your mower blade at a height of 2 to 4 in. (5 to 10 cm), your grass will be able to retain more water and grow lush.

Get your mower blades sharpened once a year so you make a clean cut. This is healthier for your grass blades. Mower shops can sharpen your lawnmower blades for you. Home sharpening kits for push mowers are also available from mower shops or places that sell tools.

Leave clippings on your lawn

Leave your mower clippings on your lawn to provide it with great nutrition—clippings are full of the nitrogen that grass loves. Clippings left on your lawn also help it retain water. If you have healthy soil, with lots of micro-organisms, these clippings will decompose. If the clippings don't decompose within a month, consider spreading some quality compost on your lawn, or spraying actively aerated compost tea to add micro-organisms. (See Chapter 9, The Wonders of Compost, for more information.)

Apply compost and actively aerated compost tea

Spreading a thin layer of quality compost over your lawn, also known as top dressing, will add soil micro-organisms and organic matter and provide nutrients for your lawn (see Chapter 4, Eco-maintenance, for details). Spraying your lawn with actively aerated compost tea will build the ecosystem of micro-organisms that feed your lawn (see Chapter 9, The Wonders of Compost).

Water wisely

When you water your lawn, put a small container out. When it has collected 1 in. (2.5 cm) of water, you will know you have watered enough. A Frisbee will fill up just the right amount. This will encourage your grass to grow deep roots, making it stronger and less dependent on water and added nutrition.

If your lawn is made up of hardy grass types, or if it has rained, you may not need to water. Otherwise, watering once a week is enough.

Changing Our Perspective on Grass

Most of my clients won't water their lawns; they consider it a waste of water. They accept the natural brown look that grass has on the Canadian prairies for most of the year.

Aerate if needed

Aerate your lawn if the ground seems to be hard and compacted. To know if your soil is compacted, try shoving a screwdriver into your lawn. If it takes much force, you have compacted soil.

Usually aeration is done in the spring. It can also be done in the fall. Avoid aerating in the summer heat because it will dry out your lawn.

You can rent an aerator at an equipment rental outlet or hire a landscaping company to aerate your lawn. Rental aerators are quite big and heavy; you need a strong person to operate these machines.

Be sure to choose a core aeration machine, which cuts little round plugs out of your lawn to allow water and air down to the roots. The plugs are left lying on your lawn and break down in a week or two. The plug holes should be at least 2 in. (5 cm) deep to be effective.

Spike aerators that work by stepping on the bar and pushing the tines or spikes attached to the bar into the soil tend to compact the soil at the end of the spikes. Therefore they are often not as effective at improving the soil structure as core aerators.

It's often best to aerate the day after a rain or watering because the ground is the right softness. After aeration is the ideal time to top dress your lawn by spreading compost. The compost is able to mix deeper into the soil as it fills in the plug holes.

Build Soil Structure to Avoid Use of Polluting Aeration Machines

Aeration machines are gas-powered. Like other landscaping machines, they are responsible for a lot of pollution and greenhouse gases. Overall it's best for the environment to use compost and aerated compost tea to build the soil structure so your lawn doesn't need aerating. Or have less lawn!

SUMMARY

- The Kentucky bluegrass lawn became the norm for urban yards through fashion and marketing.
- Kentucky bluegrass lawns are not environmentally sustainable in most climates—in hot, dry conditions they require water and fertilizing.
- Having other features besides lawn, or minimizing lawn area to where you use it, is the most eco-friendly and low-maintenance way to go for your eco-yard.
- By overseeding, you can gradually change the grass types in your lawn to those suited to your yard.
- Keep your lawn lush and healthy by mowing high, leaving grass clippings on your lawn, applying compost and actively aerated compost tea, watering wisely and aerating if necessary. ·

NOTES

1. Much of the history information in this section comes from Liz Primeau, *Front Yard Gardens: Growing More Than Grass* (Toronto, ON: Firefly Books, 2003). The xeriscape history comes largely from Sara Williams in the book cited in Note 3 below.

2. Carole Rubin, *How to Get Your Lawn and Garden off Drugs*, 2nd ed. (Madeira Park, BC: Harbour Publishing, 2003), 14.

3. Sara Williams, *Creating the Prairie Xeriscape: Low-maintenance, Water-efficient Gardening* (Saskatoon, SK: University Extension Press, University of Saskatchewan, 1997), for the xeriscape and water use information.

4. Michael Alavanja and Matthew Bonner, "Pesticides and Human Cancers," *Cancer Investigation* 23 (2005): 700–11.

5. Lance P. Walsh et al., "Roundup Inhibits Steroidogenesis by Disrupting Steroidogenic Acute Regulatory (StAR) Protein Expression," *Environmental Health Perspectives* 108 (2000): 769–76.

6. Sophie Richard et al., "Differential Effects of Glyphosate and Roundup on Human Placental Cells and Aromatase," *Environmental Health Perspectives* 113 (2005): 716–20.

7

Making Beds to Replace Your Lawn

Earth laughs in flowers. —*Ralph Waldo Emerson*

Ciliates

One of my purposes in this book is to support you in replacing your lawn with other landscapes that are more environmentally friendly and sustainable. Depending on your eco-design, you might plant some combination of flowers, vegetables, shrubs and trees. It can be easier than you think to remove a lawn and replace it. Here are some methods.

COVER-OVER METHOD

Cover-over is the easiest method and the friendliest to the environment because it leaves your existing soil ecosystem intact. This method is also known as "smothering" your lawn. Except for the mulch delivery (which you would probably get anyway) it requires little or no machinery.

The cover-over method simply involves covering your lawn with newspaper or cardboard, then a thin layer of compost to enrich your soil, then a thick layer of mulch. Later you can plant through the mulch. Newspaper tends to work better than cardboard in drier climates, as cardboard dries out more easily. The newspaper blocks light and the

Digging out the sod at the edge of the bed

Placing the sod to make a raised bed

Covering the lawn with overlapping newspaper

mulch blocks air from the grass so it will die, decompose and become lovely organic matter to nourish your new plants!

Here are the steps:

1. Mark the boundaries of the area you will cover. You can use landscape chalk, string, a hose or extension cord.

2. Dig out about 1 foot (30 cm) of sod at the edges of your bed. This is so the grass won't come up later along the edges. You can place the sod on top of the lawn in the middle of your bed to make a raised bed or you can remove it (see What to Do with the Sod later in this chapter).

3. Cover the lawn with newspaper at least half a newspaper (15 sheets) thick. I like to use a full newspaper for thickness. More newspaper won't hurt, and less may mean grass comes through. Overlap the covering layers by at least 6 in. (15 cm) so that grass and weeds don't poke through. Wetting the cover can help to hold it down, especially on windy days.

4. Spread 1 to 2 in. (3 to 5 cm) of compost on top of the newspaper or cardboard. It can help to lay a small section of cover first, then

Wetting the newspaper to hold it down

Spreading compost over the newspaper

Spreading wood chip mulch over the bed

Wetting down the bed once complete

the compost, wetting the cover as you go, especially if it's windy.

5. Spread a 4 in. (10 cm) layer of mulch over the compost. Wood chips often work best for mulch as they won't blow away. You could mix leaves and some grass clippings or other organics in with the wood chips if you like.

6. Wet the whole covered-over area thoroughly to soak it through. You should need to do this only once.

The Eco-yards Crew Works This Way:

- One person removes all the glossy flyers and opens the newspapers so they are fully open in a wheelbarrow.
- One or more people spread the newspaper out on the lawn, laying down one full open newspaper and then overlapping it halfway with another full newspaper.
- One person sprays down the laid-down newspaper to keep it wet, keeping the hose turned on and using a spray nozzle that sprays only when squeezed.
- One or more people dump the compost on the newspaper with wheelbarrows.
- One person rakes the compost flat.
- One or more people spread the mulch.

We don't have a crew of 15! Folks do double duty: for example, the compost raker or newspaper opener can also be the newspaper wetter.

Depending on where you are mulching, you may want to install edges to hold in the mulch. Edging could be something like rock walls, bricks or boards. Note that wood chip mulch pieces do tend to stick together, which may allow you to simply taper the height of the mulch down along the outer boundary, rather than actually build up an edge. In that case, lay down more thickness of the newspaper or cardboard along the edge to really prevent the grass from poking through.

Ideally, you would do this cover-over in the fall, let the microbes do their decomposing of the grass over the winter and plant in through the mulch in the spring.

If you do want to plant right away, you have a few options:

1. Cover the newspaper with 4 in. (10 cm) of composted soil or compost/soil mix rather than with 1 in. of compost. This will be enough to plant small plants above the newspaper or cardboard layer. Plant and then put down your mulch.

2. Dig holes for larger plants before you cover the lawn, making the holes about 5 in. (7.5 cm) wider than usual. The wider holes will help prevent grass from coming up around the plants. Put pots or buckets upside down in these holes to mark the holes and keep them from filling up with compost. Then spread your newspaper or cardboard cover. Leave a 5 in. (7.5 cm) space free of cover around your plants so water can easily get to their roots. Then spread your compost/soil. Plant, filling the holes around the larger plants with compost/soil. Then put down your mulch.

3. You could also dig through the mulch and cover to make planting holes—it's just a bit more work. I either use a really sharp shovel, jumping on it to get through the cover, or I pull back the mulch and cut the cover away with a utility knife. Again, leave the 5 in. (7.5 cm) area around the larger plants free of cover.

Buckets placed in holes where larger plants will go after spreading soil

Cutting through newspaper cover with a knife to plant

The lasagna variation

A variation of the cover-over method is to build soil on top of the cover. This is called the lasagna method. On top of the newspaper or cardboard cover, spread layers of compostable materials, alternating green and high-nitrogen layers (grass clippings, kitchen scraps, rotted manure) with brown layers (finished compost, leaves, wood chips). Use one part green material to four parts brown material and build it up about twice as deep as the roots of the plants you wish to plant on the cover layer. After settling and composting, the material will end up about half as thick. (For details on what's "green" and "brown," see Making Compost in Chapter 9, The Wonders of Compost. For more on the lasagna method, see Chapter 12, Growing Vegetables.)

To plant, just pull away the compostable layers, fill the area around the plant with composted soil or compost/soil mix and plant on top of the cover. For larger plants that need deeper holes, use option 2 (above), digging out the holes before you start.

You can then cover your "soil to be" with 4 in. (10 cm) of wood chip mulch.

Gathering Materials for Making Lasagna Soil

The lasagna method of cover-over requires materials you may not have immediately available. In this case, you can cover small sections of your lawn as materials become available. Or you could gather all the necessary materials first. For example, in the fall you could gather leaves and/or grass clippings from around the neighborhood, pick up some well-rotted manure from a local farmer, get a load of wood chip mulch delivered and build your beds to decompose over winter.

The leave-it-a-long-time variation

I have done the cover-over method with leaves in a sheltered spot, gathering bagged leaves from alleyways in the fall. I laid down cardboard, put a 14 in. (35 cm) layer of leaves over it and let the area sit for a year.

I moved from that house before I was able to plant anything—the area was still covered in leaf mulch and had only a few strands of quack grass growing up between the cardboard overlaps. It would take a few years to become soil. Mixing in grass clippings or other greens would have speeded up the soil-building process.

Where to Get Newspaper, Cardboard

You could save newspaper and cardboard yourself, ask your neighbors to save it for you or take a trip to the recycle depot or bin and pick some up. For a whole yard, you'll want a lot of newspaper, so start collecting it or scout out where to get it well before you start your cover-over project. For cardboard, I have scoured back alleys for appliance boxes and the like.

Where to Get Mulch

You can purchase mulch. It's much cheaper to buy it in bulk at a landscape supplier or nursery than in bags. You can also call an arborist or your local power company to see if they will deliver mulch to you—they remove trees and chip them. Some community composting facilities give away wood chip mulch.

Using carpet to cover-over

Many gardeners use carpet to cover-over because large areas can be covered quickly. I know acreage owners who are effectively covering over their thistle patches with carpet. Because it stays in place, carpet also works well on slopes. Used carpet is available for free and would just end up in the landfill, so why not use it for your yard? The one reason not to use carpet is that most carpeting contains toxic chemicals. Avoid using it near vegetables, herbs or other plants from which you will eat.

Otherwise, use carpet just as you would cardboard or newspaper. Usually, you turn the carpet upside down and then cover with compost and mulch. Where you want to plant, use a really sharp knife to cut a

A boulevard covered over with carpet and planted with hardy perennial flowers

planting hole through the carpet. Although carpet will take a few years longer than newspaper or cardboard to decompose, the soil micro-organisms will chew up the carpet and transform the toxins—microbes eventually turn almost anything into soil.

Solarization

Solarization is a method that involves using the sun's heat to cook and kill plants (usually grass and weeds). Solarization involves covering an area of plants with dark plastic, preventing airflow under the plastic by putting weights along the edges and middle of the plastic. This method is effective in warm climates with warm nights, which excludes most of Canada and the northern United States, especially the Northern Great Plains.

You need to leave the plastic on for at least a few weeks. If temperatures underneath it get high enough (at least 150°F or 66°C), weed seeds will also be killed. Once the vegetation is dead, you can plant in it. If you want to improve the soil quality, you can top it with compost before planting. Once planted, cover it with mulch.

DIGGING SOD OUT BY HAND

To remove your lawn, you could dig the sod out by hand. People can be hired to do this—it does not take much skill, mainly a strong back and strong arms. Be sure to dig deep enough to get out the grass roots—this is usually about 6 in. (15 cm).

To release soil from around the grass roots, you can turn the sod chunks over and let them dry. Then bang them together or against your shovel. I like standing on the sod chunks and smushing my boots around on them to release the soil. This step is not necessary,

Sharpen Your Shovels

Keep your shovels sharp to make your digging easier. Use a round file to scrape at a slight angle (enough to slide a thin knife blade under at the high end) along the tip of the shovel. Do many quick strokes for a few minutes. You probably only need to do this from the inside of the shovel.

although it does keep more soil in place and makes for less sod to haul away.

SOD STRIPPER AND ROTOTILLER

You can rent a sod stripping machine. About the size of a large rototiller, it requires a big, strong operator. A sod stripper will only dig 4 in. (10 cm) deep at the most, which is not usually enough to get out all the grass roots. When I use a sod stripper, I usually add compost to the soil left in place and then rent a rototiller to chew up the remaining grass roots and mix the compost into the soil. I place wood chip mulch on afterwards, and for the next season, some grass may grow through the mulch, especially near the plants where the mulch is in a thinner layer. Then I just manually pull or dig the grass out.

While refraining from tilling or digging is usually best for the soil, in some situations tilling is the best option. Adding compost helps restore the soil microbes, especially fungi, that have been chewed up by the rototiller.

EXCAVATING WITH MACHINERY

You could use a bobcat (a small excavator) or hire a company that does excavation to dig up your lawn. Some considerations:

• If you are having the sod hauled away, you will also need to hire a trucker unless the company you hire has both excavation equipment and trucks.
• If the equipment has to cross lawn, that lawn will be damaged by the wheels or tracks—pretty much unavoidable. If it is lawn you want

to keep, you can repair it afterwards by adding soil and grass seed (preferable because you can plant hardy grasses) or re-sodding that area. Be aware too that the heavy excavation equipment will compact the soil, which is not so great for soil and grass health.

- Make sure the equipment can access the area you are wanting to have excavated. Some companies have mini-excavators, which need only a 36 in. (92 cm) wide space to pass through. Most excavating equipment is wider than that.
- How deep do you want them to dig? It depends on what you are going to have there afterwards and the condition of the soil. If I'm going to be planting beds, I excavate at least 8 in. (20 cm) deep. I will speak to the excavators about where trees will be planted and have them dig deeper there (2 feet or 60 cm)). Also, I'll excavate deeper if the underlying soil is poor, say pure clay, especially if it is a small area—I've gone up to 2 feet (60 cm) deep.
- The company you hire (especially the trucker) may want to know how many cubic yards (or cubic meters) of material will be dug out. Here are the formulas for calculating that:

    length (in feet) × width (in feet) × depth (in inches) ÷ 324 = cubic yards

    length (in meters) × width (in meters) × depth (in centimeters) ÷ 100 = cubic meters

WHAT TO DO WITH THE SOD

To make more sustainable use of the sod than taking it to a landfill, lots of options are available. Here are four:

- Dig the sod up around the edges of your beds, mound it up grass-side down and make berms and raised beds that you can plant in. Use the cover-over method detailed at the beginning of this chapter.
- Stack it up in an out-of-the-way area, grass-side down, and let it slowly compost over a few years. To make it compost a little faster, you can water it when dry. You don't have to turn it, although you can if you have a strong back or an excavator. You can compost some sod along with your regular compost, but it's best to only add a few chunks at a time, because large quantities will slow down the composting process.

Keep Organic Wastes Out of the Landfill

Sod or other organics in landfills end up decomposing anaerobically, creating methane gas, which some smart landfill operators are capturing to use as fuel for other operations. Usually though, methane gas produced by organic materials in landfills is released into the air. Methane, a greenhouse gas, is 20 times as effective at trapping heat in the atmosphere as carbon dioxide, contributing to global warming. So, it's best to compost your organics! Proper composting with lots of air will not produce methane.

- If you have to haul the sod away, take it to a composting facility. Landscaping companies or nurseries that make their own compost may let you dump it in their compost pile for no charge. Some landfills have composting facilities too.
- Another option is to look for someone advertising that they want free fill. Acreage owners and farmers often want fill for their land. Let them know it is sod, though, as sometimes they won't want this. Ask them what they are using the fill for. I once took truckloads of sod to an area, then found out they might be using it to fill in part of a natural wetland. I didn't want to be contributing to that!

REPLACING THE SOIL

If you have dug up your lawn, you need to replace the soil. Soil can be purchased at composting facilities, nurseries and landscape supply companies.

Bring in soil rich in organic matter and microbes. It may be made from yard waste (say, the sod from a lawn!), woody materials, manure and other organic matter. The best soil will have been composted properly (taken to at least 150°F or 66°C for three days and worked long enough to finish composting) so that any plant seeds in it will be cooked and unable to sprout in your new beds. This type of soil is probably only available in bulk at a composting facility or nursery that makes compost. Buying in bulk and having the soil delivered, or picking it up yourself with a pickup truck, is the most cost-effective way to buy soil.

If you cannot get composted soil, then buy a mix of compost and topsoil. Very often the topsoil has come from a pile full of weeds and will contribute weed seeds. Spreading mulch thickly enough on top of the soil (at least 4 in. or 10 cm) will prevent many of these seeds from sprouting, making them less of an issue.

The topsoil may have come from agricultural land. My feeling is that it's best to use consumer dollars to support making new soil (from composting operations) rather than stripping valuable agricultural land for landscaping purposes. If topsoil from agricultural land is the only soil available to you though, it's probably better to use it than to leave your lawn in place! A more sustainable option is to use the lasagna method detailed in the cover-over section of this chapter to build your own soil.

Paver brick edging separates the lawn from the flowerbed

EDGING OPTIONS

Edging is used to keep grass that is growing beside beds from creeping into the beds. It is also used around raised beds to hold in the soil and mulch. Edging is often chosen for its decorative look.

If your beds will be next to lawn, you can edge them or not. You could just dig a trench to below the grass roots' level where the bed meets the lawn, and you won't need edging. The trench will work just as well to keep grass out of your beds.

The cheapest edging is plastic, not a sustainable material. If you choose plastic, get professional grade and use stakes to hold it in the ground.

Rocks can be used for edging, as can paver bricks, available from landscape supply companies. Paver bricks can make mowing next to beds easy—the mower wheels just run along the bricks if you place their tops flush with the lawn's surface. New methods are also available for easily making concrete edging against lawn. The most sustainable material for edging is usually natural rock or wood from your area.

MULCH

Mulch is simply something that covers the soil surface. If you look at a forest floor, you will see mulch—branches, leaves, fruit that fall to the ground—forming a layer that decays to produce new soil. This is how a natural ecosystem works, and we can work that way too in our yards.

Avoid rocks and landscape fabrics

I'm a fan of organic mulches only. Rocks raise temperatures in the soil and surroundings, do not contribute organic material to the soil, do not prevent unwanted plants from growing and are generally inhospitable to plants. Landscape fabric and plastic interfere with the natural transfer of organic matter and microbes, and they very often end up showing at the surface where they look unsightly. People often lay down plastic or fabric and rocks and then expect that area to be weed-free. It doesn't work in the long run because dirt builds up in the rocks and weeds grow in that. Weeds will also grow through tears in the plastic or fabric. It can be quite a job to remove the rocks and fabric to get to the weeds beneath.

Putting organic mulches on top of landscape fabric or plastic doesn't work because, without direct contact with the soil to which they could stick, the mulches may slip off or blow away. This is also the case when gravel or rocks are spread over landscape fabric covering a slope—the rocks slip off, leaving the unsightly fabric.

Organic mulch materials

Many organic materials can be used as mulch:

Wood chips. Chips that are about 1 to 2 in. (3 to 5 cm) in size seem to work the best in terms of retaining moisture and staying in place, rather than blowing away like finer mulches can. Larger wood chips don't seem to retain moisture as well. Wood chips are often available for free from arborists and power companies that trim trees around power lines. Call them and ask if they have a list of people waiting for delivery. Often, they will take your name and address and dump a load of chips when they have been working in your neighborhood. Community composting depots often have chips available for free also. Wood chips can be purchased in bulk from some nurseries, sawmills and landscape supply companies.

Note: Some companies are making chips from salvaged lumber. These chips are billed as long-lasting as they do not biodegrade quickly. They may have decorative value, but they are not as effective at retaining water, moderating temperature or adding organics as most other wood chips.

Leaves. Ever available, especially in the fall season in northern climes. I gather leaves that neighbors have bagged and left for garbage pickup. I use leaves for mulching my flower beds over winter and for my compost bins. I select smaller-sized leaves, so they decompose faster.

Evergreen cones and needles.

Straw.

Grass clippings (dried).

Sawdust and wood shavings. These will decompose quickly and can be helpful around smaller plants.

Post peelings. These are bark strips shaved from trees to make fence posts.

Ornamental bark chips. These tend to be expensive and don't retain as much moisture as mulches with smaller pieces.

Newspaper. If you really need mulch and have nothing else!

Organic mulch can be applied permanently to beds. Mulch can also be used seasonally. For example, I spread a layer of leaves about 5 in. (13 cm) thick over my perennial beds in the winter to protect them from the winter cold and from freeze-thaw cycles. In the spring I remove any mulch covering the plants, leaving some just on the soil, and compost the leaves I have removed. Strawberry plants are often winter mulched with straw, which is easy to remove in the spring.

Benefits of organic mulch

Organic mulch has important benefits:

Retains moisture in the soil. Mulch prevents evaporation of water from the soil by cooling the soil, protecting it from wind and acting as a physical barrier to evaporation.

Prevents unwanted plants from growing. Thousands of seeds are in the top layer of the soil. Mulch prevents them from getting the light they need to germinate. Mulch also stops weeds that do germinate from growing up from the soil or down from the top of the mulch.

Improves soil. Mulch provides organic matter for the soil. Mulch also keeps the soil's moisture level and temperature more consistent, which leads to healthier soil structure (less drying and cracking) and stimulates microbe activity. Mulch prevents soil from compacting as much as bare soil would when walked on.

Cautions for using mulch

- Wood chips and sawdust of some tree varieties (e.g., western red cedar and black walnut) contain substances that will prevent plants from growing, so avoid those types of wood.
- Wood chips from arborists or compost depots may have been sprayed with chemicals that could harm your plants. Letting your wood chip pile sit for six weeks to decompose a bit can help. Making sure you have chips from a lot of different trees can reduce the risk. Overall, the benefit is probably worth the risk.
- Some sawmills compost their wood chips for a season to ensure they are disease-free before selling them. If you really want no-risk chips, buy these.
- For people with environmental sensitivities, the smell and fungi in wood chips can trigger reactions, so you may want to use other organic mulches, or go without mulch. In this case, completely cover your beds with plants—groundcover plants can be a good filler between other plants.
- Some wildflowers not native to the the forest won't thrive with wood chips. Use straw or leaf mulch with these native wildflowers.
- Large areas of straw, evergreen cones or wood chips could be a fire hazard in some locations—you may want to use other materials there. If you are in the country far from fire services, avoid putting flammable mulch near your house.
- Mulch will prevent your flowers from spreading by seed. If you want a patch of self-seeding flowers, avoid mulching that area.
- With mulch, wet areas of your yard may retain too much moisture. You may want to plant bog plants there (without mulch) or correct the drainage in that area.
- The nitrogen depletion factor—you may read or hear that putting down fresh mulch will take nitrogen away from your plants as it decomposes. Relax! If you are building healthy soil, your plants will have lots of nitrogen available to them. The benefits of mulch far outweigh temporary nitrogen depletion.

Applying mulch

Here are the steps to follow in putting mulch on your beds:

1. Plant your plants first.

2. If you want to put soaker hoses on your beds—usually rubber hoses that distribute water throughout their length—lay them down now in a pattern that ensures they water near the drip line of every plant. The drip line is where water lands when it drips from the plant during rain—at the outside edge of the outer leaves.

3. Water the beds heavily.

4. Apply mulch 4 to 6 in. (10 to 15 cm) thick. Less than 4 in. (10 cm) won't be as effective at preventing unwanted plants. More than 6 in. (15 cm) may not let enough air into the soil. Leave some space unmulched around plants—about 4 in. (10 cm). In other words, don't put the mulch right up against the plants—they need air, and that space can prevent the trunk or main stem from decomposing. Sometimes it looks goofy to have little mounds of mulch 15 cm (6 in.) high in between many plants in a bed, so I just spread the mulch as thickly as possible while making the whole bed look good.

5. Water the mulch and beds heavily again.

Soaker hoses placed in bed before mulching

6. You will need to top up the mulch on your beds on a regular basis. This is a good thing—it means your mulch has added organic matter and nutrients to the soil. Wood chips usually need topping up every two to three years. Grass clippings and leaves may need topping up once a year or more often.

SUMMARY

- Lawn can be removed by
  - covering it over
  - digging it out by hand, sod stripper or excavator
- It's best to dispose of your sod in such a way that it will end up as new soil or compost, rather than in a landfill.
- Replace sod with composted soil if you can, or a rich mix of compost and topsoil.
- Organic mulches retain moisture, prevent weeds and improve soil.

8

Soil: A Feeding Frenzy

In the garden the door is always open into the holy — growth, birth, death. —May Sarton

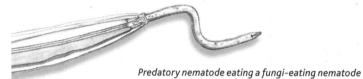

Predatory nematode eating a fungi-eating nematode

Soil is more than just dirt. In healthy soil an entire ecosystem of micro-organisms (bacteria, fungi, protozoa and nematodes) brings nutrients to plants at their roots. Plants need 60 to 80 different nutrients to be healthy and grow properly, and they actually—and amazingly!—orchestrate this swarm of microbes to bring them exactly what they need.

How? Recall that plants photosynthesize—they use the energy from sunlight to produce sugars. A plant sends 60 percent of these sugars down to its roots. A sixth of that is used to feed the roots while the rest is exuded from the root walls in the form of specific sugars, carbohydrates or proteins (converted by the plant) to feed microbes — in fact, to feed the exact types of microbes that will provide the nutrients the plant needs at that time. (The soil ecosystem also feeds and protects plants via their leaf and needle surfaces.)

If a plant requires nitrogen, it will exude food that will support many common soil bacteria. If the plant requires calcium, it will exude food to support fungi, which carry crystallized calcium. These bacteria and fungi will cluster against the root wall, absorbing the goodies the plant is feeding them and storing the nutrients the plant desires.

A constantly shifting mix of microbes competes for exudates at the root zone. The mix of microbes changes through the season as the plant alters what it exudes to satisfy its changing nutritional needs. At any one time, a few hundred species of microbes will be active. Healthy soil will support tens of thousands of species of microbes, allowing the right ones to be available when needed. (Microbes become dormant when the conditions aren't right for their species—e.g., too hot, cold or dry—and are able to wake up and become active when conditions are right.)

Bacteria and fungi are like a stocked pantry right next to the roots, keeping nutrients from washing out of the soil and always at the ready for the plants. Bacteria and fungi produce substances that help them stick to each other and to other surfaces so they themselves won't wash away!

Bacteria and fungi are needed to store nutrients for plants. Protozoa and nematodes are needed to then release those nutrients and make them available for plants. Many of the bacteria and fungi clustered at the root wall or on the leaf surface get eaten by protozoa and nematodes. The protozoa and nematodes digest the minerals and nutrients into forms the plants can use and then excrete them. The metabolism of protozoa and nematodes actually chelates minerals—bonds each ion to

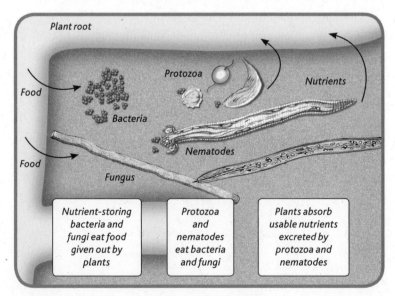

Plant root

Food

Protozoa

Bacteria

Nutrients

Nematodes

Food

Fungus

| Nutrient-storing bacteria and fungi eat food given out by plants | Protozoa and nematodes eat bacteria and fungi | Plants absorb usable nutrients excreted by protozoa and nematodes |

Plants and soil microbes work together to feed each other

a protein—thus making the minerals much easier for plants to absorb. The plants then absorb the usable nutrients through their root walls and leaf surfaces.

Roots don't make digestive enzymes that would break nutrients down into forms that they can use, so they need the microbes to do this for them.

MICROBES PROTECT PLANTS

Within a tenth of an inch (a few millimeters) of a plant's root wall, a boisterous feeding frenzy is going on! (See the drawing in the color pages.) The same kind of thing happens on leaf surfaces. The microbes are so thick along the roots and on the leaves of a plant in a healthy soil ecosystem that harmful bacteria or fungi have a hard time coming close. Many of the beneficial bacteria and fungi also produce substances that deter harmful bacteria and fungi. A healthy soil ecosystem not only feeds plants, it protects them from disease! Powdery mildew (botrytis), for example, is a common fungal disease on plants, covering the leaves with a white powder. Using actively aerated compost tea sprays, rich with soil microbes, scientists and farmers have found that they can reduce powdery mildew. (See Chapter 9, Making Compost, for more on compost tea.)

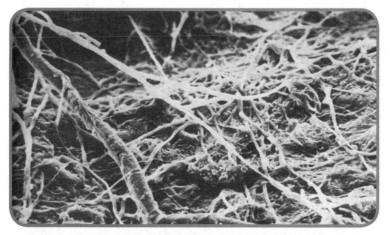

Leaf surface greatly magnified under an electron microscope. Fungi, bacteria and other microbes are so thick on it, harmful diseases and pests can't get to the leaf. (Courtesy of Elaine Ingham, Soil Foodweb, Inc.)

A Single Gram of Soil

One teaspoon (gram) of healthy soil contains:
- 100 million to 3 billion bacteria of 20,000 to 30,000 different species
- several yards (meters) of fungal strands with 30 to 100 miles (50 to 160 kilometers) of surface area to absorb nutrients
- several thousand protozoa
- a few dozen nematodes

THE MICROBE LINEUP

Bacteria

Bacteria are the tiniest and most numerous microbes in healthy soil. Bacteria live near plant roots and also throughout the soil. They feed on plant exudates and also on organic matter such as dead plants or animal droppings in the soil. Because bacteria are one-celled organisms, they digest their food outside their bodies! Through their cell walls, they release enzymes to digest the organic matter, and then they absorb the digested nutrients back through their cell walls. Bacteria can digest most organic matter, including the tough cellulose of dead plants. They are such great digesters, in fact, that they are being used to clean up oil spills and reclaim chemically contaminated land. Bacteria are the oldest life form on Earth and are essential to all life processes on Earth—all other life forms have evolved by using bacteria in their life processes.

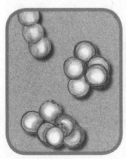  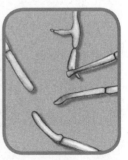

Round bacteria   *Spiral bacteria*   *Rod-shaped bacteria*

Bacteria exude slime, a sticky substance that protects them and helps them move. Colonies of bacteria, together with other micro-organisms, attach themselves to a surface and encase themselves in slime to form a biofilm community wherever the surface contacts water. You can easily see some biofilms: the gunk that clogs a drain or the gel-like coating inside a vase that has held flowers for several days. Other biofilms may be hard to see—e.g., the slippery coating on rocks in a stream, or the plaque on your teeth. Slime helps hold soil together.

Most bacteria need oxygen to live. Anaerobic bacteria, however, can live without oxygen. They often cause disease, and they produce compounds that stink (like really slimy, rotten food)! You don't want anaerobic bacteria in your yard. You would usually only notice this smell in soggy compost or in a really flooded and wet, stagnant area of your yard. This is a sign of not enough air there—you need to turn your compost—aerate it and keep it drier, or somehow get air into that wet area of your yard.

> ### Ahh, the Sweet Aroma of...Bacteria
>
> The bacteria *Streptomyces* is responsible for the good earthy smell associated with healthy soil.

Some bacteria and fungi produce acids that can dissolve rock to release nutrients such as phosphorus, sulphur and calcium. The bacteria and fungi store the nutrients until they themselves are eaten, after which those nutrients are available for plant use.

Bacteria store many nutrients and are the main storehouse of nitrogen, a key nutrient for plants. Nitrogen is the basic building block of amino acids, which are used to make proteins. Having lots of diverse bacteria in your soil means more nitrogen is available to your plants.

Fungi

Fungi are the main agents of decay in the soil. Fungi grow from spores and look a bit like tree branches. They grow fast at the tips and release enzymes there that digest organic matter. Fungi digest many of the same things bacteria do and also digest tougher woody materials (lignins and cellulose) and chitin, the material that makes up insect shells. Like bacteria, fungi then absorb the nutrients into their bodies. The enzymes fungi release continue to digest organic matter in the soil.

Fungi absorb and store many nutrients and are particularly noted for storing calcium crystals on the outside of their strands.

Fungi can grow up out of the soil to find food (e.g., up to leaf waste on the soil surface). They can also grow down to where minerals can be found. The fungi then bring these nutrients to plants through their network of strands to trade them for plant exudates at the root wall. Fungi can also bring water to plants.

When fungi die, they are eaten by other microbes, leaving passageways through the soil for air and water.

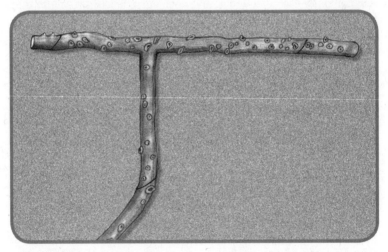

Fungal strands with calcium crystals

Mycorrhizal fungi

Mycorrhizal fungi are a special type of fungi. They look like roots and grow from within roots, extending by 700 to 1,000 times the root system's ability to reach out into the soil for nutrients! These fungi can grow out and down for hundreds of yards (or meters) to mine the nutrients and minerals the plant needs, feeding the minerals back to the plant through their fungal network. Sometimes mycorrhizal fungi

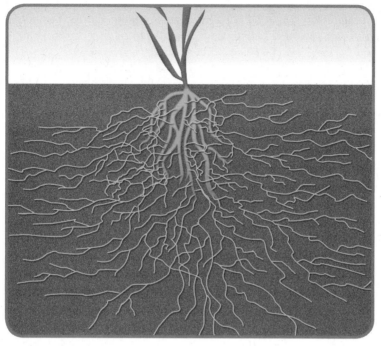

Mycorrhizal fungi extending the root system of a plant

will even take nutrients from one plant and pass them to another. About 450 million years ago, plants were first able to grow on land, thanks to mycorrhizal fungi, which started colonizing plants that grew in the water.

Mycorrhizal fungi release acids that unlock phosphorus from rocks. Copper, calcium, magnesium, zinc and iron are other minerals these fungi transport to plants. Mycorrhizal fungi are so helpful to plants,

Protecting Mycorrhizal Fungi

To protect mycorrhizal and other fungi in nature, logging practices could be adjusted to take only some trees from an area in order to disturb the soil as little as possible. Construction practices could also be changed to minimize digging and soil disturbance. For example, equipment could travel only over certain corridors. Natural vegetation and soil could be left in place as much as possible.

it's important that we steward our yards in ways that allow their fragile strands to grow and do their work. You can protect fungi by not using harmful chemicals, by tilling and digging only when necessary, by avoiding compacting your soil and by preventing areas of your yard from flooding.

Protozoa

Protozoa play an important role by eating bacteria, and sometimes fungi, and excreting their stored nutrients in a form plants can use. The three main types of protozoa are amoebas, ciliates and flagellates — perhaps familiar from your school days!

Ciliate   *Amoeba*   *Flagellate*

Nematodes

Beneficial nematodes eat bacteria, fungi and other nematodes, digesting and excreting nutrients in forms plants can absorb and use. You know you have a healthy soil ecosystem in your yard when predatory nematodes (the ones that eat others) can be seen in your soil samples when viewed under a microscope.

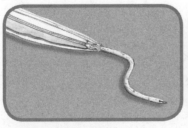
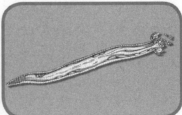

Predatory nematode eating a fungi-eating nematode   *Bacteria-eating nematode*

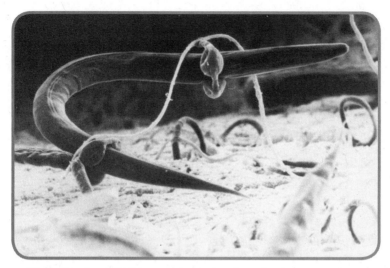

A fungus trapping a harmful nematode as seen under a microscope
(Courtesy of Elaine Ingham, Soil Foodweb, Inc.)

Root-feeding nematodes, however, which insert their spiky noses into root walls to suck out nutrients, are not so great for plants. A healthy soil ecosystem can prevent root-feeding nematodes from attacking plants such as your tomatoes. In this photo, a strand of fungus is actually trapping a root-feeding nematode!

RATIO OF BACTERIA TO FUNGI

The ratio of bacteria to fungi varies according to the types of plants in the vicinity. For example, where agricultural crops grow, bacteria and fungi are present in equal masses. In a mature forest, the fungi in the soil outweigh the bacteria ten to one. This is because in the successional process—in which weeds come first, then grasses, perennials and shrubs and finally trees—the different plants need different support from the soil. For early successional plants, like grasses, bacteria provide lots of nitrogen. Trees, which appear later, require what fungi can bring.

In your yard then, the grass and annual flowers and vegetables will be happy with lots of bacteria. Manure-based composts are great for supplying bacteria. If you have perennials, shrubs and trees, you will want to support good fungal growth in your yard. You can do this by adding woody materials to your compost and putting wood chip mulches on your beds.

It's usually more challenging to encourage more diversity and abundance of fungi in your yard than bacteria. Even annuals and grass require some fungi, so I recommend using compost made with some woody materials on your yard.

MICRO-ORGANISMS CREATE SOIL STRUCTURE

Micro-organisms create soil structure too! The bacteria create slime that glues soil particles together. Fungi are in long threads that hold soil particles together. Larger organisms—like earthworms and little mites—carry nutrients around and create air passages as they burrow through the soil. Good soil structure with lots of air passages allows microbes, water, air and nutrients to move through the soil. Structure also helps the soil hold water and nutrients, making for healthy plants.

WHAT HAPPENS WHEN CHEMICAL PESTICIDES ARE APPLIED?

When chemical pesticides are applied to plants and soil, microbes die. The leaf and root surfaces of the plants are less protected, and the plants cannot get the nutrients they need.

Applying compost and actively aerated compost tea restores the microbes and the natural soil ecosystem.

WHAT HAPPENS WHEN CHEMICAL FERTILIZERS ARE APPLIED?

When chemical fertilizers are applied to plants and soils, grasses perk up right away, or seem to, because they get a big dose of nitrogen. Perennials, shrubs and trees can't absorb the most commonly used nitrate fertilizers, so they don't receive any benefit. Some of the soil microbes dehydrate and die due to the salty nature of the fertilizer. Larger organisms, like earthworms, migrate away from the irritating salts of the fertilizer. The fertilizer that's not immediately absorbed by the plant roots washes into the water system, where it often wreaks havoc, causing algae blooms and sometimes making water undrinkable. Using chemical fertilizers seems to decrease the organic matter (carbon) in the soil too.

Chemical fertilizers often contain only three minerals: nitrogen (N), phosphorus (P) and potassium (K), in various ratios. Plants need 60 to 80 nutrients, including micro-nutrients like selenium and manganese (important for producing seeds), to be healthy. A healthy soil ecosystem, rich with microbes and minerals, supplies the nutrients plants need far better than chemical fertilizers and without side effects to the environment.

Organic fertilizers are better than chemical fertilizers but a poor substitute for the rich mix of soil microbes and nutrients found in good compost. And microbes are still needed to make the nutrients in organic fertilizers available to plants.

WHAT HAPPENS TO THE SOIL ECOSYSTEM WHEN WE TILL AND DIG?

When we till and dig, the valuable fungal strands are broken up, air passages that carry oxygen to microbes collapse, and the soil loses life. It's better to dig only when necessary (e.g., to plant something or to work compost into really depleted soil). Generally it's best to add compost on top of your soil. If you have mulched beds you can rake back the mulch, put the compost on top of the soil and then replace the mulch. Even if you put the compost on top of the mulch, the microbes and nutrients will still find their way into the soil.

IT'S TIME TO RESTORE THE LIFE IN OUR SOILS

In the last 100 years, chemical and mechanical practices (tilling) have greatly depleted soil microbes around the world and thus the health of our soils upon which we depend. It's time to restore the life in our soils. Compost and actively aerated compost teas are an effective way to do this. (See Chapter 9, The Wonders of Compost, on how to make compost and compost tea.)

AMENDING SOIL CHEMISTRY

Restoring soil health may require more than just restoring a healthy ecosystem of microbes. Restoring soil chemistry may be important too. Scientists who take an organic approach to improving soil have a range of ideas on what to do about balancing the minerals naturally found in healthy soil. Heavy use of chemical fertilizers usually puts mineral balances out of whack. Most scientists say that restoring the soil microbes is key to restoring mineral balances (and it may take a long time). Some say mineral imbalances can continue even in a restored microbial ecosystem. The debate is about how best to measure what's needed to balance the minerals and how best to bring balance. I still have much to learn in this area; for now, here is my best advice:

• If you are willing to be patient, build up your soil biology with compost and actively aerated compost teas and leave it at that.

• Look at the signs in your yard—if the plants are doing well, you don't need to do anything. If you have lots of "weeds" (e.g., dandelions, quack grass), it almost always means that your plants aren't able to get enough calcium from the soil and probably not enough phosphorus either.

• Many soil experts who ascribe to the approach of this book say calcium is the gatekeeper needed for plants to grow. Others say that adding calcium to your soil will correct essential mineral imbalances in your soil. And all agree that soil is complex, so be cautious when adding just one mineral.

• If you do want to add calcium, use the most natural form you can. Calcium carbonate (lime) and calcium sulfate (gypsum) are two good variations that can be found from natural sources.[1] Which you use may depend on whether your soil also needs carbon, available in calcium carbonate (lime), or sulfur, available in calcium sulfate (gypsum). If you add calcium over a few years, switch types so that you're not overloading the soil with carbon or sulfur. It is better to add a bit at a time than a lot at once.

• Fungi are needed to hold calcium in the soil and to make it available to plants, so if you are adding calcium, also add fungi-rich woody compost or actively aerated compost tea.

- You can have your soil chemistry tested. A water soluble mineral test will tell you what minerals are available to plants at the time you took the soil sample (this will vary throughout the growing season and from year to year, so the test will only reveal what your plants need right now). An exchangable/extractable mineral test will tell you what minerals are in the soil (these may or may not be plant-available). If you find a difference between what is available in the soil and what is available to plants, rather than add more of the missing mineral, add compost to put the microbes to work making the nutrients available to the plants. You can also have the micro-nutrients tested.

- Some labs will do all these tests. Labs use different methods, so if you want to see how your soil is changing over time, choose a reputable lab and stick with it. You can find labs in the Yellow Pages or on the Internet, usually under Soil Testing.[2]

- The lab will recommend what minerals you may need to add, usually in pounds per acre. The typical urban yard—on a lot 50 feet wide by 125 feet deep and not including the area covered by the house—is about one ninth of an acre, so you would divide the lab's recommendations by nine.[3] Some labs also have "home gardener" packages that make calculating what you need easier.

- Elaine Ingham, a renowned expert in soil biology, is leery of adding chemical fertilizers directly to the soil. She advises putting $1/60$ of the amount of mineral recommended by a lab test into your compost pile and letting it work there for at least two weeks. The compost processes the minerals so they are usable to your plants and won't harm your soil. Then you can spread that compost over your lawn or beds. This is a good approach if you want to be cautious.

- If you haven't had your soils tested, but from looking at the state of your plants you think they could use some mineral aid as well as more microbes, you can add some natural minerals to your compost pile and let them work two weeks. Add lime (calcium carbonate), soft rock phosphate (phosphorus) and rock dust—rich with micro-nutrients. These probably won't hurt anything and could really speed up your soil restoration. Then spread the compost on your yard or make compost tea with it to spray on your yard.

- If you have been using lots of chemical fertilizers, you may want to transition slowly to organic care so your plants don't suffer withdrawal! Halve the amount of fertilizer you use each year over two to three years, while you also use compost and/or actively aerated compost tea. Switch to organic fertilizers. Alfalfa pellets, fish hydrolysates and kelp-based products are all good. Humic and fulvic acids are also great to use with fertilizers and compost as they make nutrients more available to plants.

- While you can search the Internet for suppliers of these products, ask your local garden centers and hardware stores to carry them so they are more available to all gardeners.

- Using lots of good compost and/or compost tea is the best overall way to restore soil health. Supporting this approach by the careful addition of minerals can speed up the process.

SUMMARY

- Healthy soil has a rich ecosystem of micro-organisms and tiny organisms.
- Plants interact with soil micro-organisms, orchestrating them to bring plants the nutrients needed at each point in their growth cycles.
- Plants need 60 to 80 nutrients to grow. Healthy soil provides this much better than fertilizers.
- Chemical fertilizers and pesticides harm the soil ecosystem by killing essential micro-organisms.
- Tilling and digging also harm the soil ecosystem.
- It is time to restore soil health on the planet! Compost and compost tea are the best ways to do this.
- Done with caution and when appropriate, adding minerals can speed up soil restoration.

NOTES

1. Heidi Hermary, in her book *Working with Nature: Shifting Paradigms*, suggests that agricultural lime or hydrated lime is too caustic for soil microbes. Only use dolomite lime if you know you also have a magnesium deficiency, or you will get too much magnesium. If you use gypsum (calcium sulfate), make sure it is from a natural source. Some gypsum comes from recycled drywall and can be toxic to plants.

2. Midwest Labs is one reputable soil chemistry lab with offices in Canada and the United States. Depending on the test, it will cost from about $25 to $100 to test your soil. Many labs also offer tests for micro-organisms; I generally don't recommend them. The best testing for micro-organisms is done by the Soil Foodweb group of labs in many locations around the world. They actually look under the microscope and count the microbes. Look for their offices at soilfoodweb.com.

3. If your lot is not 125 feet deep by 50 feet wide OR the area you want to put minerals on is less than the whole lot minus the house, you need to measure the square feet of the area you want to amend. Just measure the width times the depth and multiply them together. For example, if you have an area 20 by 15 feet, that would be 20 × 15 or 300 square feet. An acre is 43,650 square feet. To find how many times that number fits into an acre, divide 43,650 by 300 = 145. So you would divide the lab's recommendations by 145 to get the number of pounds of a certain mineral they recommend you add to the area.

If you prefer metric, an acre is about 4,047 square meters. If you have an area 4 by 20 meters, that would be 4 × 20 or 80 square meters. To find out how many times that number fits into an acre, divide 4,047 by 80 = 50.6. So you would divide the lab's recommendations by 50.6 to get the number of pounds of a certain mineral they recommend you add to the area. To change pounds to kilograms you can then divide by 2.2.

COMPOST TEA RESULTS

The lawn on the left was overseeded once with compost and had compost tea sprayed twice. The lawn on the right had chemical fertilizer and herbicide mix applied.

The left lawn in the adjacent photo three years later after being overseeded once a year and sprayed with compost tea three times a year.

A yard sprayed with compost tea three times a season for two years.

A tree in New Zealand suffering from a fungal disease. This tree, sprayed three times with compost tea, recovered in six weeks. Unsprayed trees nearby showed no improvement.

Microbes at the plant root: the feeding frenzy

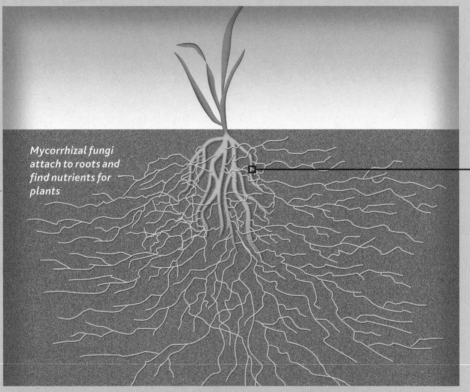

Mycorrhizal fungi attach to roots and find nutrients for plants

The Microbes

Bacteria	store nutrients......................		
Fungi	store nutrients......................		
Protozoa	eat bacteria and excrete (poop out) nutrients that plants absorb	Amoebas.......	
		Ciliates	
		Flagellates	
Nematodes	eat fungi		
	eat bacteria......................		
	eat nematodes......................		
	and excrete nutrients that plants absorb		

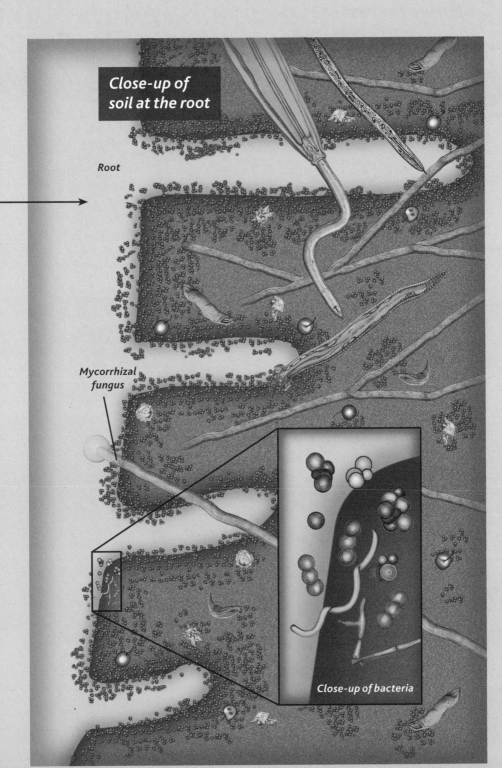

Close-up of
soil at the root

Root

Mycorrhizal
fungus

Close-up of bacteria

©2009 Laureen Rama

THE HEATHER-INSPIRED YARD

(As described in Chapter 10)

Before.

The yard has been excavated.

Composted soil has been brought in and the rock river laid.

One year after new plantings of low perennial flowers.

Three years later the perennials have spread to provide a continual feast of colour during the growing season. A creeping pine near the house adds winter interest.

FROM LAWN TO FRUITS AND FLOWERS
Cesar and Marichu's Eco-yard *(As described in Chapter 6)*

Before.

The happy work crew.

After, from the house.

Native Blanketflower and friend.

Evans sour cherries.

FRONT YARDS

Hardy bergenias bloom in spring beside low juniper

A thyme lawn that needs little or no watering

Different willows and evergreens provide winter color

Aspen poplar grove

BACK YARDS

Raised vegetable beds with flowers that deter harmful insects.

Water-thrifty plants in a tufa rock wall and in containers

Hardy and native perennial flowers bring beauty to a lawn used for play

FRONT YARDS

River of local rock with hardy groundcovers.

A vegetable garden.

A variety of plants leads to a variety of insects, supports pollinators and keeps harmful insects in check. These (below) are hardy and native perennial flowers and some self-seeding annuals that bloom at different times to provide color throughout the growing season.

9

The Wonders of Compost

Work with nature and nature will work with you.
—*Dick Kitto*

Fungal strands

I. Making Compost
(Your Eco-yard's Best Friend)

The foundation of your eco-yard is healthy soil, and the best way to build healthy soil is with compost. Good compost contains nutrients and micro-organisms that will feed your plants. Good compost also contains lots of organic matter (once alive and composed of living tissue), whose fluffy structure improves soil structure by allowing lots of air and water to move through it.

The living plants and animals on Earth are part of the carbon cycle. Plants use energy from the sun in the process of photosynthesis to turn carbon from the air into plant matter. When plant material is put into a compost pile, it breaks down, releasing the carbon and inorganic materials, such as minerals. This process is helped along by the "bio-zoo" in the soil—fungi, bacteria, protozoa, nematodes, earthworms and tiny insects. The result of the composting process is humus or finished compost.

When added to soil, compost

• lets more air into the soil
• allows more water into the soil, and keeps it available for the plants

- allows plants to grow more roots because it creates more air space and channels
- keeps the mineral parts of soil from compacting and forming hardpan, or crust, on the soil surface
- holds nutrients in the soil, making them available when the plant needs it
- adds micro-organisms to the soil

Fluffy compost on fingers (Courtesy of Elaine Ingham, Soil Foodweb, Inc.)

WORKING THE HEAP

In the old days, the compost pile was the leftover stuff from cleaning the barn (horse or cow manure and straw) and was stacked somewhere out of sight until it had aged. The farmer then applied it to a garden patch or field. In those days, everyone farmed organically! Compost happened by itself. Here's how those who want healthy, fluffy soil can make it happen faster.

A diversity of ingredients creates a compost with many nutrients and micro-organisms. The two main kinds of ingredients are known as *brown*—vegetable material that has aged and dried out—and *green*—fresh vegetable material that is still green and moist, such as grass clippings, kitchen scraps or carrot tops.

The dynamic dance of brown and green materials in proper balance, with the help of the "bio-zoo" of decomposers, produces humus. The decomposers need to live in the "Goldilocks zone" of temperature and moisture conditions: not too hot, or too cold, too wet or too dry, but "just right."

Recipe for a compost pile

- 45% brown stuff—material such as wood chips, waste straw, dried leaves
- 45% green stuff—wet stuff such as grass clippings, green plant material, kitchen waste
- 10% high-nitrogen stuff—material such as manure, alfalfa, legumes such as beans and peas
- Optional: one shovelful of garden soil to add soil micro-organisms, or a commercial compost starter

If you don't have a lot of high-nitrogen materials, the compost will still "work." It will just take longer. In three weeks to a year (depending on climate, temperature and moisture variables—the Goldilocks range), your compost will be finished.

Examples of ingredients that can be added to a compost pile:

Brown Materials
- eggshells—dry
- dead leaves—dry
- newspaper (white pages)—dry
- cardboard—dry
- dryer lint—dry
- sawdust—dry
- bread and grains (no butter, cheese or meat)

Green Materials
- grass clippings—wet
- landscape waste—wet
- vegetable and fruit kitchen scraps—wet
- coffee grounds and tea leaves

High-nitrogen Materials
- alfalfa

• legume plants, such as peas or beans
• manure—from horses, cows or sheep (i.e., vegetable consumers).
  Note that dog, cat and human manure can contain pathogens that
  may not break down in a small compost pile. Composted manure can
  be purchased in bags from your local garden center.

Kitchen waste can be collected in a covered container that's stored
under a sink or on a back porch. There are many containers on the
market that keep smells down and allow for oxygen-loving micro-
organisms to start the compost process. These containers need to be
emptied every few days. Food scraps are great for worm composting as
well. (See next section in this chapter.)

TYPES OF COMPOSTERS

Many types of composters can be used, e.g.,

• a compost pile in an out-of-the-way spot
• woven wire fencing in a circular or square shape
• wooden compost boxes
• concrete open-topped bins
• commercial plastic composters
• plastic tumbling composters

Each of these different types of composters has its advantages and
drawbacks. A simple pile of compost may look unsightly on a suburban
lot or be prohibited by homeowners' associations. Compost boxes are
inexpensive but must be constructed. Nonetheless they are handy

Plastic composter

Tumbling composters

and usually look good. Plastic composters bought at your retailer work really well, but the pile should be checked for dampness or dryness and stirred often, as air circulation is limited. Tumbling composters work well in that they are mobile and compost quickly, but can only hold so much material. Covering compost with soil and stirring often will deter animals, as will a "hot" pile (see section Hot vs. cold below). Plastic and tumbling composters are closed devices and consequently deter animals as well.

Three-bin compost system with removable front slats for ease of moving materials in and out. Top slats allow chicken wire to be placed over top to keep out animals and birds. A compost screen is on top of the closest bin.

Compost-lovers have devised many efficient systems to make fresh compost continuously available. There are the two-bin system, the three-bin system and, on a very large scale, the windrow system. In the multi-bin system, while one pile composts, another is started; when the first pile finishes, yet another pile is started to supply a continuous stream of humus to the gardener.

PLACING YOUR COMPOSTER

Place your pile or composter in an easily accessible spot near your house so that it is convenient for you to add your kitchen waste. But not too close: sometimes bins attract mice, so you won't want the composter where mice may enter your house. If you are storing leaves or other yard waste to add to the compost, make sure you have room to store these near your bin. Think ahead about how you will create and maintain your compost so you can design and place it most conveniently.

MAKING COMPOST

Layer the ingredients, alternating green, brown and high-nitrogen materials, starting with branches on the bottom to allow for air circulation. Water the pile so it is damp but not dripping or soggy, and then keep the pile damp. This may mean watering it in dry climates or covering it with a tarp or other cover in rainy areas. If you don't water your pile in a dry climate, it will take much longer to compost (e.g., two years vs. one). If your pile gets too wet, it can get stinky and anaerobic (keep reading for how to remedy this).

Turn the pile every few weeks. A good time to mix and add water (preferably from a water barrel so it's not chlorinated) is when you add

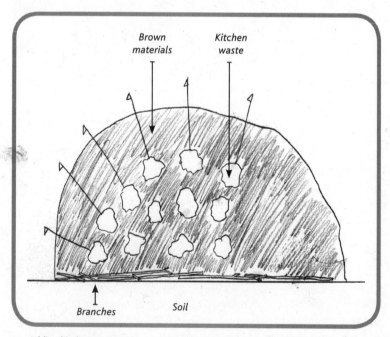

Adding kitchen waste to brown materials. Cross-section of a compost pile (described opposite).

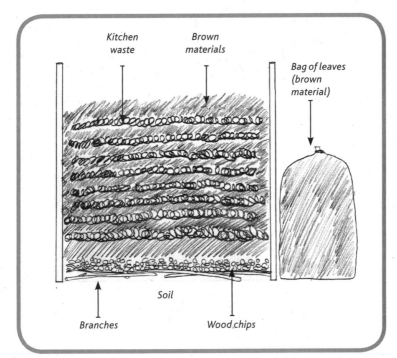

Layering kitchen waste and brown materials. Cross-section of a compost bin (described below).

more material to the pile. Depending on the climate and how favorable conditions and ingredients are in your pile, you may have compost within three weeks to a year.

If you will continually be adding kitchen waste to your household pile, you can form the pile out of brown material and insert the kitchen waste in various spots throughout the pile, preferably at least 2 feet (24 cm) deep. Some people mark the spot with a flag each time. Once the pile has no more room for kitchen waste, turn it. This is the time to add the 10 percent (by volume) of high-nitrogen material (manure, peas, beans) if you have it. The high nitrogen will cause the temperature to rise. If high-nitrogen materials are not available, the pile will still compost, but more slowly.

Another way to build a compost pile that will include kitchen waste is to start with woody materials over which you place brown materials. Keep more brown materials handy (in a separate pile or in bags or bins). Each time you add kitchen waste, spread it on top of the pile and cover it with brown materials. I collect bags of leaves in the fall and store them near my compost bin to use as brown materials. You could add high-nitrogen materials when you choose to turn the pile.

If you don't turn the pile, compost will still be created and you can shovel it out from the bottom.

HOT VS. COLD

One of the really useful things about compost piles is that they actually kill bad bacteria when they reach an internal temperature of 140°F (57°C) or more. Hot piles require a larger compost bin or pile of at least 16 to 22 square feet (1.5 to 2 square meters) to heat up. Cold piles tend to be smaller and take more time to break down the organic material.

> ### Free Heat!
>
> People are doing lots of clever things with the extra heat generated from compost piles. Some heat greenhouses. Some have installed pipe systems through large compost piles to preheat water for domestic use such as showers and radiator heating systems. This is an emerging area of "off the grid" technology.

Once a compost pile gets going, its temperature should rise to between 135°F (55°C) and 155°F (70°C) for three days, after which it will usually drop again once the high-nitrogen materials are broken down. This is the time to turn the pile, and the temperature will rise again. If it goes above 155°F (70°C), however, your microbes may die off. Compost veterans can get a sense of how the pile is "cooking" by digging right in, taking a good look and feeling it to gauge temperature. If you're not there yet, garden centers carry long thermometers to monitor compost piles.

IF YOUR PILE GETS STINKY

If your compost pile gets smelly and slimy, it's not getting enough air or oxygen. The pile is too wet—anaerobic bacteria have taken over.

The pile is telling you it needs to be stirred or turned and have more dry stuff added. Every time the pile is turned, oxygen is added and moisture is released.

TURNING YOUR COMPOST

Turning compost is an art in itself. As mentioned earlier, turn the pile of "hot" compost when it gets too hot. Be aware, though, that the fungi bio-buddies grow when the pile is cooler and still, so try to turn it as little as you can get away with. Professional compost connoisseurs like to let the pile sit for at least two weeks after the compost has finished "cooking" to allow fungal strands to reform.

Essential tools for compost turning have traditionally been the pitchfork and, recently, the pile-turning fork. For small compost bins, winged mixers are available. You shove the mixer down into the pile, the wings then spread out, and you can lift and move the compost around to stir it.

Remember that composting is a natural process and *will* happen, even if you don't follow recipes exactly and aren't able to turn the compost. Relax and enjoy the knowledge that you're *creating* soil and restoring the Earth!

CHOPPING MATERIALS

Compost piles will make humus more quickly if the organic material used in the pile is chopped or shredded. The smaller the compost material the faster the pile will break down. If you have a large yard, it can be useful to own or rent an electric or gas-powered chipper-shredder (share with your neighbors!). This is one instance where the

Compost Cleans the Environment!

A benefit of composting is that it will digest chemicals that have been used on the yard or on composted materials, usually within one season.

benefits of the result may outweigh the environmental costs (pollution, greenhouse gases, energy use) of running petroleum-powered machinery. Wood chips are great for your compost and for mulch. A larger gas wood chipper could be converted to a diesel engine and run on biodiesel. If you still have a power lawn mower, it can also be used to shred leaf litter and yard waste. You could also hand chip materials with an axe, a machete or clippers.

USING THE HUMUS

Farmers and gardeners everywhere have called properly made compost from the garden or worm composter "black gold." That's because the bio-buddies, via decomposition and enzymes, have made the nutrients bound up in the old leaf litter/food scrap pile available to nourish a new generation of garden plants—in the form of humus. And this humus is rich in soil micro-organisms.

To prepare compost for application, break the finished compost up by putting it through a screen. To make a screen sieve, nail or staple some

Compost screen

¼ in. hardware cloth or rabbit wire to a wooden frame. You can make the frame with 2 in. x 2 in. (5 cm x 5 cm) square lumber screwed together with metal corner brackets. A handy size square frame will be 24 in. (61 cm) square.

Screens can also be purchased from garden suppliers. For example, Lee Valley Tools has carried a small rotary screener, handy for small compost batches.

Screened and dried compost can be applied to a lawn with a seed spreader. This works well for spreading worm compost as well.

Screened compost can also be raked over the lawn with a leaf rake. Buckets of compost can be added to soil mixtures and potting mixes and applied as a top dressing on the soil around flowers, vegetables, shrubs and trees. (See Chapter 4, Eco-maintenance for more on spreading compost.)

Composting keeps microbes fed, contributes to the available nutrients in your yard, reduces organic matter going to landfills (where it creates methane, a greenhouse gas) and contributes greatly to the organic gardening process, which keeps the soil nutrients and bio-zoo in the yard and out of the waste stream. All of this creates ideal growing conditions for plants that provide food and shelter for pollinators, other wildlife and you! This in turn contributes to the biodiversity of your neighborhood, bioregion and the world, restoring the natural ecosystem.

II. Worm Composting
(by Caron Wenzel and Laureen Rama)

AS THE WORM TURNS

Remember the old saw: "Feed the soil, not the plants"? It is well-known among organic gardeners that, to feed the soil, worm compost is one of the best. Worm composting (vermicomposting) is ideal all year round, and you can have your wiggly friends live indoors or out—under the sink, in the basement, in any space that might otherwise be wasted.

You won't find red wiggler worms (*Eisenia foetida*)—two to three inches long and a dark red—in the back yard. They are native to

> The plough is one of the most ancient and most valuable of man's inventions; but long before he existed the land was in fact regularly ploughed, and still continues to be thus ploughed by earth-worms. It may be doubted whether there are many other animals which have played so important a part in the history of the world, as have these lowly organized creatures.
>
> – Charles Darwin, 1881

A Worm by Any Other Name

Some folks are finding that European night crawlers (*Eisenia hortensis*) are tougher than red wigglers, able to take a wider temperature range and better at handling stress.[1]

temperate rain forests. Rather than burrow into the soil as earthworms do, red wigglers eat and live on top of the soil, in the "litter" layer of the forest floor, helping to decompose leaves and other debris and creating the humus layer that makes the forest smell so nice. Being temperate climate critters, red wigglers like the same temperature ranges we humans do; they usually won't survive cold winters. Laureen does, however, now have red wigglers in her outdoor compost bins in the winter. She has found that piling leaf bags on them provides enough insulation—they survive the winter in these bins. During the summer, she puts the red wigglers in her leaf bags and then uses these semi-composted leaves as bedding for her worm bin.

Available at your local bait shop, one pound (half a kilogram) of red wiggler worms will get you into the compost business. Red wigglers are super-critters! They have five pairs of hearts, no teeth or bones; they can reproduce three months after hatching and live for up to 16 years. They eat constantly (especially lettuce and cantaloupe), including any newspaper bedding they live in. They don't sleep, are hermaphrodites and lay eggs. In fact all they do is eat and have worm sex. What a life! Incredibly, these worms have enzymes in their intestines that can change really toxic stuff (toxic even to humans) into good soil. Possibly even more amazing is that they don't carry or transmit any known human diseases. Super-critters indeed.

Treat Your Worms Like Livestock

Worms are pretty easy to care for, but they *do need* care. Materials need to be turned, and food and bedding added every few days. If you're not prepared to do this, better not to get worms! When Laureen travels, she takes her bin to a friend's house or has someone come over to feed the worms.

Worm bin

SETTING UP A BIN

The average 10-gallon (40-liter) or larger opaque plastic bin is ideal. With a medium bit (¼ in. or 6 mm) on your electric drill, put 20 or so holes in the lid of the bin. This is easier to accomplish if the lid is on tight. Remove plastic filings, wash the bin with soap and rinse very well. Turn the lid upside down and duct-tape plastic screening under the air vents you have just drilled so the worms cannot get out. If you put vent holes in the bottom, the bin will have to be raised onto blocks and set in a tray to catch the liquid that leaches from the bin. This prevents the bin from getting too wet.

Leaves Make Great Bedding Too

For Laureen's large outdoor worm bin (placed in the garage with a small lid heater in the Canadian winter), she uses dried leaves as bedding. These leaves have been partly composted in the bags by adding some water and some red wiggler worms! Composting the leaves a bit is important so that in the summer heat they don't start freshly composting and cook your worms!

Food for Worms

Do feed your worms

• fruit, vegetables, grains, stems, peels/rinds, cores, seeds, coffee grounds and filters, tea bags, bread crust, pasta, soggy cereal, lettuce, paper towel

Don't feed your worms

• meat, cheese, bones, gravy, salad dressing, oils, butter, salted food, plastics, metals, glass

Go easy or avoid using

• orange, lemon, grapefruit peels

Place about 3 to 8 in. (8 to 20 cm) of bedding in the bin to start. Bedding for red wigglers is really easy and cheap. They love shredded newspaper. A paper shredder works well or you can tear newspaper into 1 in. (2.5 cm) strips lengthwise. Paper egg cartons and corrugated cardboard boxes are tasty bedding too. Soak these in water (non-chlorinated is best) and then wring them out before placing in the bin.

What worms need

Red wigglers have gizzards like chickens to "chew" their food, so you have to add a handful of garden soil or sand to aid their digestion. Wigglers

Worm Wow-factors

• Worms are nocturnal.

• Direct exposure to sunlight can kill a worm in three minutes.

• Worms breathe through their skin.

• The first third of the body contains vital organs, the remaining two thirds contain intestines.

• In a bin, a wiggler consumes half its weight daily.

• One pound (half a kilo) of worms, comprises 1,000 worms.

• Red wigglers are fair-weather creatures; they like temperatures in the 55°F to 85°F (13°C to 29°C) range.

need calcium to make eggs, so boiled eggshells, pulverized to a powder, should be added weekly. Calcium carbonate (lime), available from garden centers, can substitute.

Lightly chop food for your worms and feed them by burying the food scraps under the bedding. This is important. Worms are light shy, and unburied food will attract other decomposers you may not want. Freezing the food first will aid in the faster breakdown of your worm food. The list on the opposite page is good for regular compost too.

Three to six months later...

Worms go right to work, and three to six months later, you will be able to harvest your "black gold." Open the bin and shine a bright light into it. Wigglers don't like light and will move down into the bedding. Scoop off the top layer of compost. A trowel works well. Keep doing this until you have removed as much compost as you need. When mostly worms are left, add more fresh bedding and food, soil and eggshells or lime. Check through your "black gold" for more worms and eggs (tiny golden spheres) and return them to the bin.

Worms create clean soil! Strong enzymes in their gut dissolve organic materials including harmful bacteria. Compost and worm bins are actually ecological systems on a tiny scale. Other critters help the worms return nutrients to the compost. In a balanced bin or compost pile, many other decomposers are present. Sowbugs, protozoa, fungi, bacteria, springtails and other good guys are aerobic digesters. If you see them, know that they need to be there.

COMPOST HAPPENING FOR YOU

Caron and Laureen have kept worm bins for ten years with great success. The compost is especially good for container gardening — our houseplants love the stuff. However, it's better not to use pure worm compost—too rich. A good mix is one part compost to two parts garden or potting soil. Top-dress potted plants with ¼ in. (0.5 cm) of the compost every six weeks or so, and they will thrive!

There's Nothing Like a Nice Cuppa Tea

Many of my clients have commented that their trees seemed richer and fuller and had fewer diseased leaves after compost tea spraying. Clients have also commented that their plants are healthier and grow larger, their yards have fewer weeds and their lawns need less watering.

III. Actively Aerated Compost Tea

Spreading good compost all over your yard is the best thing you can do for your yard. But it can be time-consuming, expensive and sometimes impractical. Enter actively aerated compost tea—the quickest and least expensive way to add soil micro-organisms to your yard. It is about the only way to add microbes to the leaf surfaces of your plants. (Spraying compost tea has even helped some gardeners bring diseased trees back to health. See the color pages for photos.) Regular applications of actively aerated compost tea will keep the microbe levels and diversity high in the soil and on your plant leaves.

Actively aerated compost tea is made by adding quality compost to water and heavily aerating it (blowing air into it) with a pump for at least 24 hours. This process will foster an explosion of microbe reproduction, creating a rich soup of micro-organisms to spray on your plants and soil. Foods for the microbes, such as humic acid and kelp, can be added to the tea while it's being brewed.

Spraying compost tea   Laureen's compost tea tank and sprayer

You may have heard of compost tea made by putting a bag full of compost into a rain barrel or a bucket and letting it sit. This tea does have lots of nutrients but it won't have the microbes—most cannot live without oxygen. The liquid that may run out of your compost bin (leachate) is also rich in nutrients, but not in microbes. Only actively aerated compost tea has beneficial soil micro-organisms.

HISTORY OF ACTIVELY AERATED COMPOST TEA

Forms of compost tea have been around since the beginning of agriculture. In the late 1970s, some Americans started experimenting with active aeration. The story goes that scientist Elaine Ingham's neighbor in Oregon made actively aerated compost tea, and it worked magic on his roses. Dr. Ingham began to study it in 1990. Her studies and interest grew, and she is now one of the main proponents of actively aerated compost tea through her international network of Soil Foodweb labs, whose research is mainly directed towards the use of actively aerated compost tea on agricultural crops.

SPRAY SERVICES

Since 2006, I have offered a service spraying people's yards with actively aerated compost tea in my hometown of Calgary. You may be able to find such a service in your area. Encourage any yard spray services you call to consider offering actively aerated compost tea— the world needs more healthy soil micro-organisms!

MAKING YOUR OWN

You can make actively aerated compost tea for your own yard. You just need some good compost and a compost tea brewer. A 5-gallon (20-liter) brewer will easily make enough tea for your urban yard. Ideally you can use compost made from your own yard waste because you will be increasing the micro-organisms that are best adapted to your local climate and ecosystem. If you don't make your own compost, obtain a good-quality compost that's made locally. Good compost has a wide diversity and high count of microbes. Best is one

> **Compost Stew**
>
> I mix a few different composts for my tea: my own worm compost, yard waste compost and some local compost made from horse barn manure and wood chips.

that has a woody component to promote fungal growth. Your tea will only be as rich in microbes as the compost used to make it.

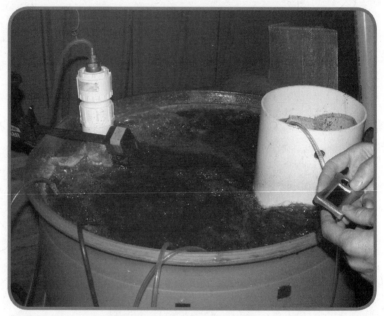

Laureen brewing 50 gallons (200 liters) of compost tea

Recipe for a 5-gallon (20-liter) batch of tea

• 2 pounds (1 kilogram) of compost (use a measuring jug: 1 liter or 1 quart of volume is about 2 pounds or a kilogram)

To feed the microbes, add:
• ¼ c. (2 oz. or 60 mL) fulvic or humic acid
• 2 tsp. (10 mL) yucca extract
• 2 tbsp. (1 oz. or 30 mL) liquid kelp (or a touch of kelp meal)
• 2 tbsp. (1 oz. or 30 mL) fish hydrolysate

These additives, and hydrogen peroxide to clean your equipment, are usually available in small quantities at hydroponic garden stores. They can order in some of the other additives if they don't have them (e.g., yucca). Large quantities of these additives are available from online sources. The additives are food for the micro-organisms in the tea brewing process and once they are sprayed on your yard. You don't need all these additives—they just make for a richer, healthier soup of microbes. Do not add molasses, as recommended by some authors. It creates too bacterial a brew.

PREPARING YOUR COMPOST FOR THE TEA

To promote the growth of fungi, protozoa and nematodes, you can prime your compost before brewing. Stir oats into your compost up to about 10 percent of the volume you have, so about 3 oz. (100 g). Quick Quaker oats work best for me; some experts say stonecut oats are best. Add enough of your liquid ingredients to bring the compost mix to about 50 percent moisture. Let the mix sit for four to seven days, stirring only a few times (you don't want to break up the fungal strands).

THE COMPOST TEA BREWER

Ready-made brewers can be found online. There you can also find instructions on how to make your own brewer.[2]

MAKING COMPOST TEA

If making tea with chlorinated water, remember to let it bubble with air for two to three hours so the chlorine evaporates before adding your compost. Put your heater in now (if you need it). Don't fill the pail of your brewer to the top—leave at least 6 in. (15 cm) of space to account for bubbling and foaming.

Put your compost in a mesh bag or paint strainer and add extra ingredients (if you use them) or have leftovers from preparing your compost. Let your tea brew for 24 hours at about 68°F (20°C).

If the mixture temperature is lower, brew a few hours more. If the liquid foams, you can add a bit of olive oil on top to keep the foam down.

Once the tea is done, take the compost out and set it aside (you can add it back to your compost pile). Leave the air pump going and take the tubing and diffusers out of the pail (so they don't backflood with compost tea). Once the tubes are blown out, you can turn off the pump.

Strain the tea through a fishnet into another clean container.

SPRAYING YOUR TEA

To spray your compost tea on your yard, you can use a small handheld sprayer found at local garden centers. Just make sure you get a big enough nozzle for fungal strands to pass through and so it doesn't clog (at least 35 mesh or 400 micrometers). Don't use a sprayer that has been used to spray chemicals. Some authors recommend using a concrete sprayer, which is about the same size as a garden sprayer and less likely to clog.

If you have a little sump pump (a clean one!), you can pump the tea through your garden hose on to your lawn, trees and shrubs. Spray the tops and bottoms of your plants' leaves as much as you can. For spray effect, I use a little plastic hose end spreader and widen about a third of the holes with skewers. The standard recommended spray rate is 20 gallons (75 liters) of tea per acre for your soil. That is about 2 gallon (8 liters) of tea for a standard city-sized yard. If you are spraying the leaves of shrubs and trees too, then use 4 gallons (16 liters) or more for an urban yard. I dilute the tea with non-chlorinated water (from the rain barrel or bubbled to de-chlorinate for an hour) so I have more volume of tea to spread over my whole yard.

Whatever sprayer you use, use the least pressure possible. The microbes are alive and can get pulverized and squashed if they hit the soil or leaves too fast.

If you live where ultraviolet sun radiation is strong, it's best to avoid spraying plant leaves between 10 a.m. and 3 p.m. The microbes take from 15 to 30 minutes to attach to the leaves, and UV rays may fry them before they can. This is not so important when you spray your soil, however, as microbes will burrow down into soil pretty quickly. You can spray too while it's raining, though the microbes may wash off the plant leaves if the rain is strong.

You cannot spray too much tea—it's all great for your yard!

Spraying once a month is optimal during the growing season and three times a growing season is enough. It's good to spray in the spring to get things going. Spraying in late fall will help the decomposition of organics, like leaves.

CLEAN YOUR EQUIPMENT!

Cleanliness is the key to long-term success with compost tea brewing. Otherwise, nasty biology will grow on your equipment and harm the good stuff. Scrub off all the parts and soak any diffusers and your tubing in hydrogen peroxide at about 8 percent strength at least overnight. Most hydrogen peroxide you buy at hydroponic stores is 35 percent, so dilute it to a quarter of that strength. Rinse everything really well and allow to dry.

SUMMARY

- Actively aerated compost tea is a quick, effective way to add micro-organisms to your yard.
- Your tea is only as good as the compost you make it with, so use compost from your own yard and/or compost with a good diversity of microbes.
- Five gallons (twenty liters) of tea can go a long way—offer some to your neighbors! Introduce them to the magic of soil microbes!

NOTES

1. Jolly Farmer Products Inc. in New Brunswick, Canada, now raises and sells European night crawlers rather than red wiggler worms for fishing bait and composting. They note this on page 13 of their 2009 catalog.

2. Five-gallon (20-liter) brewers are not as available as larger-sized brewers. At the time of writing, five-gallon brewers were available from jollyfarmer.com. For other sources, search online for "compost tea bucket brewers."

For instructions on making your own brewer, there are a few online sources. You can try my website: eco-yards.com. Authors differ on the employment of air diffusers in the brewer. If you have a large enough pump and are willing to soak the diffusers in hydrogen peroxide, they're fine.

If you're in a cooler climate and brewing outside, you'll need an aquarium heater for your brewer. Some instructions don't mention this because their writers are from warm southern U. S. states.

Pet or aquarium stores will usually have everything you need to make your brewer, except the bucket and a paint strainer bag (for the compost). Hardware stores have 5-gallon (20-liter) pails with lids. You can get a paint strainer bag at a paint store.

10

Designing Your Eco-yard

One more small piece of the
world won to beauty.
—Judy Barilla

Amoebas

**It's important that the design of your eco-yard be pleasing
to you and your household and also in harmony with the
neighborhood. Ideally your neighbors will be pleased with
it too, or at least not displeased!**

Tastes differ, so your eco-yard will probably be unique to your taste
or the combined tastes of those in your household. This is good
news! Rather than laying out specific designs, this chapter will
suggest questions you can ask yourself to guide your design
process, along with some general guidelines and considerations
for design.

HOUSEHOLD HARMONY

In my experience, it usually is one person in a household who
primarily has the vision and desire for an eco-yard. If you are
operating solo and can make all the decisions yourself, that's great!
If your household includes others—a partner, children, friends or
relatives—it's important to share the design process with them
too. They may have needs or desires that can be incorporated, as
well as preferences and dislikes. You want the design to create

harmony in your household, not present a source of ongoing annoyance. So taking the time upfront to work the design out with others can make life easier as your eco-yard develops.

NEIGHBORHOOD HARMONY

If you are going to do something like plant a wildflower meadow in a front yard where there used to be lawn, it's a good idea to let your neighbors know your plan and especially the reasons behind it. They'll be more likely to appreciate your yard and less likely to complain to municipal authorities. Most municipalities have guidelines for what is allowable on your property. It's a good idea to check the bylaws or ordinances before you begin, to see what's allowed. These can often be conveniently researched on the Internet. If what you'd like to do is not allowed, you may be able to get special permission or to work with your politicians to have the laws changed. As eco-yards become more popular, municipalities have been relaxing their laws to allow for more natural designs.[1]

CLARIFY YOUR INTENTIONS FOR YOUR ECO-YARD

Why do I want an eco-yard?

Ask yourself: is my main goal to be more ecologically friendly or simply have less yard maintenance? Do I want to co-create more beauty, or do I need a summer project? Getting really clear on your reasons for starting an eco-yard or moving toward one can help you stay motivated during the process and clarify your priorities for your yard.

How can my eco-yard harmonize with my lifestyle?

What is your lifestyle, or what do you want it to be, and how do you envision your eco-yard supporting that? For example, if you have small children, you may want play areas in the yard that can be turned into other features once the children grow older. If you work full-time and spend your weekends out hiking or camping, you may not want to devote time to a vegetable garden. Lower-maintenance plantings would be the way to go. If you have physical challenges or are getting older, yet you love puttering in the garden, you may want to plant raised beds that require little bending to tend.

CLARIFY YOUR RESOURCES

How much time and money are you willing and able to put into your eco-yard initially and on an ongoing basis? If you have lots of money but little time, you may want to hire someone to design and co-create your eco-yard.

Budget

How much money are you willing to spend on co-creating your eco-yard? This is really important to determine before you start, as costs can add up quickly. Your desires may overreach your pocketbook, so being clear on your budget can help you and/or your designer establish parameters for the process. Beautiful gardens can be created with little money.

Time considerations

Design and co-creation
• How soon do you want your eco-yard to be completed?
• How much time are you willing and able to put into designing and co-creating your eco-yard? Do you have other people who want to help you?
• Are you wanting to create your eco-yard step-by-step over a few years?

Maintenance
Do you want an easy-maintenance yard, or are you willing to spend a few hours a week gardening and looking forward to it? This is a key design question. I ask my clients who want easy-maintenance yards if they are willing to do half a day of clean up in the spring and a few hours a month during the growing season. If they are, the design can be more flexible in terms of the plants chosen than if they want to spend only a few hours a year. All yards, no matter what the design, require some maintenance.

CLARIFY YOUR AESTHETICS
(WHAT YOU FIND BEAUTIFUL)

What do you find beautiful? Are there colors, shapes of trees and flowers, forms or structures, smells, sounds, textures that delight you?

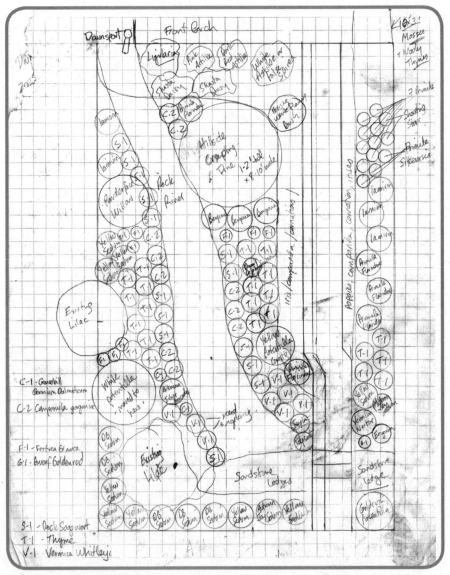

The heather-inspired yard plan (see the description on the opposite page)

If it's challenging to answer such questions off the top of your head, use local resources to uncover what you find beautiful. Look at books or magazines that contain lots of garden photos. Travel around your city or town and look at your fellow citizens' yards. Take a camera on your visits (I take mine with me most of the time now to snap photos of yards) so you can remember and compare features later. It can also be helpful to take notes. What it is about that yard or feature that is pleasing to you—is it the color? shape? the juxtaposition of features? materials used? the lines? the size?

In addition, in most urban centers, garden shows and tours put on by local horticultural societies are wonderful opportunities to talk to other gardeners and see what can be done in your area.

Color

What are your favorite colors? What are your favorite color combinations? Are there are any colors you don't like?

At the time I designed my first flower garden, I often went hiking in the mountains. I looked in wildflower meadows for colors that were

Taking Inspiration from Heather

One client of mine wanted to take out all the lawn in his front yard and replace it with something eco-friendly. He had not thought much about what he wanted it to look like; he was relying on me to come up with an idea. I showed him *Front Yard Gardens: Growing More Than Grass* by Liz Primeau, a book containing hundreds of photos of various plantings in front yards across Canada. He stopped at one photo—a yard carpeted in low groundcovers. He said he liked it because it reminded him of the heather on the moors in Scotland where he grew up. So we designed using only plants shorter than 12 in. (30 cm), chosen for their various blooming times so that, all season long, colorful blooms were visible from the front room and the front porch where he sat to play his guitar. For winter color, I planted a creeping Scotch pine that will eventually be nine feet wide and only a foot tall. See the color pages for photos.

pleasing to me. I also noticed the color palette of Rocky Mountain wildflowers—which colors were represented and in what combinations. I was happy to note that my favorite color at the time—purple—was often found in mountain meadows in various shades and hues, particularly the softer lilac tones. Purple flowers were usually contrasted with yellow flowers. White and blue flowers were also found and occasionally bright red, salmon or fuchsia Indian paintbrush. I planned my perennial flower garden to have a mix of bulbs, wildflowers and cultivars that were lilac and yellow, with some blue, white and the occasional red for flare. As a consultant, I worked at home and would often take breaks to gaze out the window at this garden—I found the colors soothing and uplifting.

You can find whole books written on color gardens—gardens planted in only one color. Would you want that? If so, what color? It is possible to create a single-color, ecologically friendly, diverse, native plant garden, even though such a garden would be a rare find in nature!

As most plants are green, are there any shades of green you like better than others? In conifers, for example, colors can vary from almost-blue to silver, dark green, light green and gold-green. Do you like a mixture of shades? How do you feel about variegated foliage in which the green is splashed with silver or gold?

Light

How much sunlight do you need or want to be happy? Are you a shade lover? Do you want to create some shade in your yard—maybe in a place where you would like to sit?

Shape

Are there plant shapes you like or particularly don't like? Very often with my clients, I've found their reason for liking or disliking a particular flower was its shape—or that of the leaves or plant as a whole. Here are some questions to think about regarding shapes.

• Do you like lily-shaped or trumpet-shaped flowers?
• Do you like daisy-shaped flowers?
• Do you like drooping flowers? E.g., echinacea has a daisy-shaped flower in which the petals droop or hang down. Other plants have a

stalk of flowers that has an arc to it.

- Do you like weeping trees? E.g., it's possible now to get all kinds of trees that weep because they are grafted or bred to hang down rather than growing up.
- Do you like the shape of conifer trees (wide at the base and narrow at the top)?
- Do you like spiky leaves? round leaves? heart-shaped leaves?
- Are there landscape forms and shapes you like or don't like?
- In nature, most forms are curved lines. Do you like curved lines? Do you like circles? Do you like straight lines? rectangles? squares? triangles? hexagons? spirals?

It's your yard—you can design with almost any shape you want. I had a friend who did her potato patch in a spiral form. Another friend makes beautiful willow trellises that incorporate a variety of geometric shapes. You could hang shapes as mobiles. You could paint different shapes on backdrops.

If shapes are pleasing to you, you may want to learn more about sacred geometry—the science and art of geometric shapes. Most feng shui systems attribute elements to the shapes; you could use shapes to augment elements that may be helpful in your yard and in your life (see feng shui section below).

Sound, scent, topography

Do you want berms—low hills that can be built into your landscape? Do you want to have different levels of land?

Do you like a wild and natural look, perhaps a little shaggy and rough, or a tidier look? Having a tidy yard does not necessarily mean more maintenance; it can be as simple as choosing tidy plants.

Do you like plants that move with the wind, e.g., tall grasses?

Do you like certain sounds, like trickling water or rustling aspen leaves? I'm a great fan of poplars because I love the sound of their leaves in the wind. In my region, poplars are the only trees that make that sound.

Do you like scents? Would you like pine scents in your garden? Floral scents? Tangy herbal scents?

Are you a fan of certain textures? Some people love the feel of grass on their bare feet or against their skin when lying down. Others love the look and feel of shiny-leaved plants, or soft fuzzy plants.

Materials

What materials are you fond of—wood, rock, water, metal?

If you love wood, you could have beds with wooden walls, wooden sculptures and chairs. Chairs and sculptures could also be metal. Rock can be used as a feature (e.g., boulders) or as material for pathways and walls.

Would you like to have a water feature in your eco-yard? Would you like to hear the sound of running water, or would you rather have still water, such as a pond? Is it the sound of water you want or the look and feel?

Using feng shui principles, you may want to balance the various energies of the elements in your yard by using different materials. Most yards with lots of plants already have a lot of wood energy, so materials made of other elements can be helpful. (See the section below on feng shui.)

HIRING A DESIGNER/LANDSCAPER

If you decide to hire a designer/landscaper to help you design and/ or co-create your eco-yard, look for a designer/landscaper who understands and follows the principles of eco-yards. The main distinction to look out for here is a sensitivity to the environment and designing using native plants.

Look for a good design rather than just fancy drawings, and if possible, hire the same person/company to do the design and the landscaping. As a landscaper, I've yet to see a design by someone else that I would use unchanged. And I've heard similar sentiments from other landscapers. What I generally find in these designs is that plants are placed too close together for their long-term size, and quite often, the species chosen are not hardy enough. The client may have spent a fair sum for nice drawings, but the real-life garden they represent isn't so feasible. I spend time and energy explaining how the design needs to change, then redesigning, and the client ends up paying twice.

I've also had a situation in which I was hired to do the plantings, the soft landscaping, after another landscaper had done the hardscaping (patio, waterfall and pond). The hardscaper did not exactly follow the plan, leaving far less room for the plants than originally intended. I was obliged to redo the plan, coming up with alternative plants.

Ask to look at a portfolio of the person/company's work. Most designers and landscapers have photos of yards they have done. Take a look to see if they appeal to you, if you like the person's style. You could also ask if you can visit the yards to see how they feel to you. One client hired me after visiting another yard I did and experiencing a peaceful feeling. If you do this, remember to give the designer/landscaper some leeway, taking into account that he or she was tailoring the style to the wishes and aesthetics of a particular client. And don't forget to ask for references of previous or current clients.

Talk to some people who have hired the landscaper before. Ask:

• Did the landscaper understand what you wanted? Did you get what you wanted or perhaps something even better than you imagined?
• How was working with the landscaper? Did they communicate well? Were they available to answer phone calls? Were they pleasant? (This may not be so important to you if they did a great job.)
• How did the landscaper handle timing and budget issues?

Be clear on your budget for the project and tell the landscaper what it is. Also share what you are willing to pay if that extra will mean the landscape will meet your intention even more (e.g., be more eco-friendly, more beautiful). These two budget guidelines—what you *want* to pay and what you are *willing* to pay—are very helpful to the landscaper in designing and planning the project.

If you have no idea about what your project might cost, or just want to get a better sense of cost, chat with your landscaper about ranges of costs, e.g., what could we do for $2,000, for $5,000, for $10,000, for $50,000, for $100,000? When I don't know what the client wants to budget, it's a challenge. Landscaping can be expensive, and I can pretty easily design either a $100,000 project or a $1,000 project. If the client doesn't give me guidelines, I'm guessing.

Hire someone you trust and be honest with them about your budget.

ECO-YARDS DESIGN PRINCIPLES

The central idea in the design of eco-yards is to support and enhance the natural ecosystem. Many types of designs may fulfill that intention.

Sample of ecosystem

You could have a sample of your local or regional ecosystem in your yard (e.g., coastal rainforest, native prairie, aspen forest). This does not mean just letting it go wild. It's a partnership with nature. For example, in some yards where lots of spruce seedlings sprouted up (largely due to the squirrels that harvested the abundant spruce cones), I dug or pulled up most of those seedlings and transplanted them elsewhere. Some tiny seedlings I laid down to compost in place. If left on their own, some of those seedlings would have grown right beside the house and blocked the entrance to the backyard. In another case, I removed all the spruces to the south of a house—they would eventually have blocked all winter sunlight.

In nature, animals prune and thin out plants by eating them or trampling them (just ask anyone who lives where there are moose and deer!). Animals also create natural pathways. As the steward of your little piece of natural ecosystem, you can do things like prune, thin, replant, move plants, weed invasive plants and create natural clearings or treed areas to co-create a space that works for your household.

Beds of native plants

You may have a more conventional layout to your design (e.g., some lawn, a patio) and still have beds of trees, shrubs and flowers that are mainly native plants or native cultivars.

- *Native* plants grow naturally in an ecosystem. Plants are considered native if they grow naturally within 300 mi. (500 km) of your locale.
- *Cultivars* of native plants have been bred from a native plant, usually by selecting for certain traits that make the flower more colorful or yield more abundant fruit.
- *Hardy* plants aren't necessarily native to your ecosystem, yet they will thrive in local conditions—the moisture levels, temperature range, wind or lack of it and type of soil (e.g., sandy, clay, lots of organic matter).

Landscaped areas or beds are more eco-friendly than lawn or hardscaped features

Why?

- Landscaped areas include a wide variety of native plants. Native plants feed native pollinators. Having native plants in our yards helps to preserve the genetic diversity, richness and beauty of plants in the wild by supporting pollinators (e.g., the Cerambycid beetle that pollinates wild roses and many other flowers).
- A wide variety of native plants also helps to increase diversity in our yard's ecosystem, an important factor in the overall health and vitality of the ecosystem.
- Landscaped areas soak up more water than lawn or hardscaped features. This helps replenish underground aquifers and prevents overload of municipal storm sewer systems and urban flooding. Natural plantings or beds can also be more water-wise than conventional lawns because you can choose plants that won't need watering after a year or two, once they're established.
- Plants restore oxygen to the air. People breathe in oxygen and breathe out carbon dioxide. Plants do the reverse—they breathe in carbon dioxide and breathe out oxygen. We need plants in order to have oxygen-rich air. This is one reason it is so important to preserve the world's forests and keep lots of plants in our towns and cities.
- It's easier to add lots of compost and organic matter to beds than to lawn. This restores the soil and its all-important micro-organisms.

Food production

Less transport of food means a lighter load on the environment. The most local source of food can be your yard! Consider berry, fruit and nut trees and bushes. You could also plant vegetable beds or plant vegetables and herbs in your flower, tree and shrub beds.

You may be surprised how many native food-bearing plants grow in your region!

Minimize work and energy use

If you want to take the eco-yard concept to its logical conclusion, look up some resources on permaculture. Bill Mollison coined this term in the 1970s to mean permanent agriculture, or sustainable agriculture. He focused on designing ways of farming that imitate and co-create with nature to make maximum use of the land, with minimal input in labor, fertilizers and gas-powered machinery for high output of food and firewood.

His design principles have been adapted to urban settings. The idea is to place features in ways which optimize return for effort. A greenhouse set against your house and near a door, for example, can both provide heat to your house and make for the least effort on your part to enter and leave. For the same reason, an herb and kitchen garden is best situated near the kitchen (given the proper sunlight and conditions). Permaculturists have also pioneered sustainable systems such as using greywater (waste kitchen water or handwashing water) to water the outdoor plants.

A suburban neighborhood development in Davis, California, was designed according to permaculture principles. The yards generally open to each other and to common green spaces. Almond trees grow throughout the neighborhood. Community vegetable gardens provide a way for neighbors to visit and have fun together, as well as providing delicious organic food. There are common play areas and lawn for picnics and play, as well as lovely hardy shrub and flower beds. Neighbors are very friendly and, especially the children, visit from one house to the other. The development harvested the almonds for sale and actually made money for their garden! People love to live there, and it's rare that a home in that neighborhood comes up for sale.

Leave a wild place

Machaelle Small-Wright, in her books and audio works on co-creating with nature (e.g., *Perelandra Garden Workbook*), suggests having one place in the yard, if only a tree or corner, that you leave completely alone. This leaves a place free for nature to do its own thing. Small-Wright would say this is a place where the devas, elves or nature spirits can rest and play. It can be a way to remember your respect for the natural world.

FENG SHUI DESIGN PRINCIPLES

"Feng shui" is a Chinese term meaning "wind water," and has come to mean the art of placement in design to allow for balance and flow. Good feng shui helps you to feel comfortable, secure and energetically balanced in a yard. Many believe that our home and yard reflect our lives and vice versa. So having a beautiful yard with pleasing proportions and a good feeling about it will help you in all aspects of your life! This is common sense.

Almost every culture has some form of feng shui, especially Asian cultures. I have learned mainly from classical and modern Chinese schools and also been influenced by Balinese and Indian forms. I still have much to learn. A few of the basic principles have been invaluable to me in co-creating yards people love. As with any design principles, these are simply guidelines; the most important thing is to design for what is most pleasing to you.

Designing for flow

One feng shui consultant invites her clients to imagine 50,000 gallons (200,000 liters) of water pouring into the yard from the large "river" of water represented by your front street. You want this water to flow in a leisurely manner to every corner and through your yard. The idea is to re-energize your yard by guiding energy gently in and throughout; you do not want it to be blasted by a tidal wave. It's also important to attract the energy and give it a way to enter your yard.

• Have some attracting features in your front yard to draw energy (attention) to your yard—sculptures, wind chimes (be mindful of neighbors—ask if they like the sound of the chimes, or have quiet ones), eye-catching plants, mobiles hanging from a tree.

• A front walk is best if it curves to your front door. A direct line from the street delivers energy too quickly and directly. It's better too if the front gate or entrance does not lie directly in line with the door.

• Place pathways or throughways to the various areas of your yard. If these can be curved, to guide energy gently through your yard, so much the better.

• Create hidden areas you can easily get to, but cannot be seen from the front or back door. This encourages exploration, drawing flow to those hidden places. If there can be delightful finds in those areas—a beautiful statue or sitting area, for instance—this adds further vitality.

• Keep your front yard low in profile (i.e., plantings low in height) so that energy has a place to pool near the front door. This energy pool is then available to enter the house through the front door. Have a lip of something a little higher at the front of your yard to hold the energy pool in. For example, you could have low groundcover plants in the main area of your front yard and plants about a foot high along the edge. A low hedge or wooden fence (e.g., made from sustainably sourced scrap cedar) could run along the front of your yard, as long as it allows entry for the energy from the street.

Designing for balance and security

Chinese schools of feng shui suggest that taller, more solid features go at the back of your yard. This helps to ground the yard and can help you feel secure, like a back rest for the space. So tall trees, rock and stone features are great at the back of your yard. It can also feel good to have taller features at the sides of your yard, with those comparatively taller to the left side of your house (if you were looking out your front door) and those that are shorter to the right.

 Balance the light and dark areas of your yard. Think of the yin-yang symbol and its equal sections of light and dark, each with a spot of the other in the middle. If you can, it's great to balance the number of darker, shaded areas in your yard with the lighter.

Brighten really dark, shadowed areas with light-colored or variegated foliage plants or lights. In a really sunny area, you could plant a darker bush or tree.

Designing for clarity

In her book *Feng Shui in the Garden*, Nancilee Wydra shares the following five points to design for clarity, meaning a comfortable familiarity with the forms of a yard that can help you feel at home.

Create edges, a border of some kind, that defines the perimeter of the whole yard. This can also be applied to certain areas of the yard. Plants, fences and walls are ways to define spaces.

Create pathways to encourage use of each area of the yard.

Create a threshold, a welcoming feature to an area of the yard or the yard as a whole. An arbor, a trellis covered with flowers or stone pillars/ceramic pots on either side create an entrance.

Create a depth view, allowing people to see at least some way into the distance so they feel comfortable with where they are and with continuing up through the yard.

Create a heart or focal point. A heart is a feature that attracts us and defines that area of the yard. For example, a boulder, a play set, a water fountain, a beautiful bed of flowers could each form the heart of variously functioning spaces. Some areas may have more than one heart—e.g., a vegetable garden and a picnic table placed in a child's garden.

Blocking undesirable energy

Protect your home and yard from strong weather (usually winds that come mostly from a certain direction) with trees, fences or walls. Think about how large the trees will become. Plant them far enough away from the house so that if they are blown over, your house will still be safe.

If you have something that you can see from your house that bothers you, such as an unsightly building across the street, plant something or put up a feature to block your view of it.

If your yard is at a T-intersection or in a cul-de-sac or curve in which the traffic points right at your house, a lot of energy is directed straight at your home. Plant or put up something that will block that energy. A large flowering bush or a section of fence or wall will work and still allow energy flow into your front yard. If a house is along a busy road, I like to plant some medium-to-tall bushes along the front; this adds a lovely entryway and some clear, open space by the door so that energy can still enter and pool there.

Working with the elements

- A water feature is well sited in front of your house. This could be a fountain, even a little free-standing one. These are available now with solar-powered pumps. Gravel can substitute for water—a small gravel patch with a statue for interest, or a gravel walkway, could represent water.
- Heavy stones are better at the back of your house and represent Earth energy.
- A firepit will bring in the element of fire. So will lights.
- Metal and wood are represented by those materials.
- Geometrical shapes, considered by some to represent the elements, could be placed strategically through your yard:
    rectangle = wood
    curves or wavy lines = water
    triangle = fire
    square = Earth
    round = metal

Healthy plants

Keeping your plants healthy is an important principle in feng shui because doing so reflects a healthy life and outlook. It's important then to choose plants that are hardy for your yard. Place them in conditions that are favorable to them (such as the amount of sunlight and moisture) so they will grow well. I have had clients who want to grow plants they love, even though conditions were not favorable in their yards. Over the years, I have realized that it's more beautiful, life-affirming and kind to see a plant thrive in existing conditions than struggle from year to year. Consider the benefits struggling plants will bring as compost, give them a worthy death and replace them with healthy plants that you love!

Attract life to your yard

Birds, insects and wildlife all bring life and energy to your yard. Consider erecting bird feeders, making little home areas for reptiles or installing bat houses, or choosing plants that attract butterflies. (See the Resources section at the end of the book for books on this topic.)

Cures for problem features

If by now you're thinking you'll have to bulldoze your yard and start again because the tall trees or rock garden in front of your house don't follow these principles, rest assured. When the physical features cannot easily be changed, or it's not desirable to change them, you can introduce feng shui cures to make up for these features and balance the energies. Examples of cures are small mirrors or lights, a beautiful object, a strategically placed fountain.

I lived in a house with three mature spruce trees in front, each 20 feet (6 meters) wide and 60 feet (20 meters) tall. The trees blocked energy from entering the yard. On the advice of a feng shui consultant, I hung colorful spiral mobiles from the trees to attract energy to the yard. Near my front door, I installed a "pool" of shiny stones and built a small rock river that flowed from the front edge of the yard to near the front door.

Feng shui is such a rich field, these principles are just a starting point. Sometimes I incorporate other aspects of feng shui, depending on the situation. For example, some feng shui schools draw a correspondence between areas of your yard and aspects of your life (e.g., career, family, health). Using a feng shui map, you can place special features, colors and shapes in those areas to enhance those areas of your ife. Note that the maps used for yards are often different from the maps used for houses. If you want to work with feng shui in more depth, many books, classes, websites and consultants are available to support you.

DESIGN CONSIDERATIONS

Designing as a Gardener

When I first visit a yard to design for someone, I usually begin by standing across the street or at a distance. I reflect on how this yard could fulfill its highest potential for beauty in harmony with the steward's desires—I've usually talked to them over the phone already and have a sense of their intentions. I stay still and let my intuition flow, getting a sense of the yard. I begin to experience visual images and hear sounds, such as children playing or birds visiting and get a sense of how the yard might be. This kind of intuitive design process is fun and can streamline the design process.

Then I talk with the stewards about their vision and share the ideas that came from my initial engagement with the yard. Usually the vision that came to me is what we design, or it is held as a longer-term vision to work toward and the design takes the yard partway to that.

Identify the main features first

Once you get down to designing, list the main features you want in your eco-yard, for example:

- beds of trees, shrubs, flowers
- section of native ecosystem (e.g., tallgrass prairie)
- deck/patio
- vegetable garden
- herb garden
- lawn
- play area
- playhouse
- eating and cooking area
- firepit
- meditation area
- garden shed
- compost bins
- fences, walls

For actual design, I use squared-off (like a graph) paper in 11" × 17" or letter-sized sheets. I use a mechanical pencil, a little template that helps me draw circles and an engineer's or architect's rule with different scales. If I want to add color, I use pencil crayons. Sometimes I will make cut-outs of certain features so I can move them around on the page. While I do design work to have a break from my computer, many landscape design programs are available for use on the computer, if you prefer.

When you design, I suggest you start with some rough, freehand sketches of what you want, keeping in mind any design guidelines mentioned in this chapter that work for you. When you're ready to draw your plan, draw in the main features first, then add the larger plants, such as trees and large bushes. Draw in perennials and annuals last.

Design as though you were writing a piece of music

Consider designing your yard, especially the plantings, as if you were writing a piece of music. Musical composition usually includes both repeated and varying patterns in melody and chorus.

You can use repetition too, in the plants or groupings of plants you place in your yard, and vary the melody in between—pleasing to the eye and the soul. For example, at the entrance to your yard, you could have a group of brightly colored plants, the same grouping halfway to your door and then again close to the door, perhaps staggered on either side of a walkway. This will draw the eye gently to the front of the yard and lead visitors to your door, as well as guide them out. In this repeated grouping, you could place plants that bloom in different periods so that color is always present in your repeated chorus.

Note that the brightest colors (red, orange and yellow) will draw your eye. Plant these colors where you want people to look and at the farthest point in any view to draw the eye through the yard. For strong notes or chords, consider mass plantings—large groupings of the plants, either all the same or a few different types together.

As in a musical composition, you can also vary the tempo in your yard. The journey through your yard could be marked by slow movements you have planted (quiet spots with muted, soft-colored plants with little

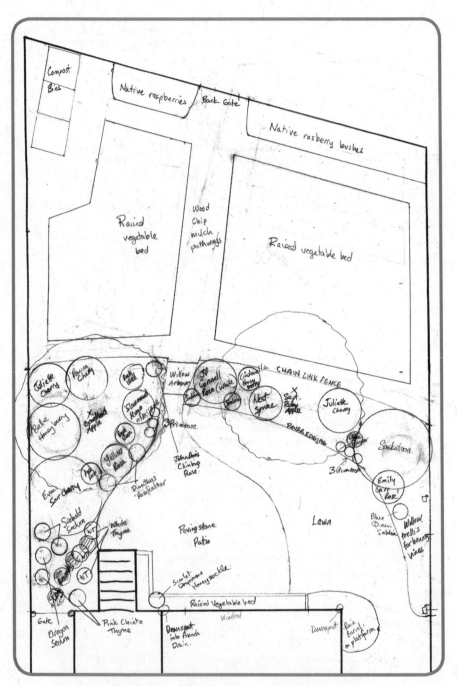

Eco-yard design plan – edible back yard (see the description on the opposite page)

variation) followed by fast movements, characterized by a wider variety of brighter, louder plants—all flowing together to create a complete melody.

You could even consider composing in a minor key! One method might be to introduce a contrasting theme in a single part of your yard. One of the most delightful front yards I've seen was planted with hardy perennials and interesting grasses with a deck and stunning water

An Eco-yard Design

Opposite is the design for an edible back yard that is south-facing in a new development in Calgary. The inner yard features apple and cherry trees, berry bushes, hardy shrubs and perennial flowers, a large trellis for climbing beans and flowering vines and lots of room to plant annual vegetables in the beds. The raised bed against the house produced over 60 large tomatoes, several hundred cherry tomatoes, 7 green peppers and a tasty eggplant—pretty amazing for Calgary! The patio is made with local paving stones. Log slices from arborist-cut trees make a pathway through the wood-chip mulched bed on the left. A lawn for the owner's small dogs was seeded with low-maintenance grass and a chain link fence built to keep them in the inner yard.

The outer back yard has raised vegetable beds made with sustainably-sourced logs, wood chip mulch paths, two native raspberry patches and a three-bin compost system made with re-used and sustainably-sourced lumber.

This is a water-wise design. A large rain barrel collects roof water from the right downspout. The other downspout goes into an underground French drain (see Chapter 11, Water-wise Design) that empties roof water into a rock well near the Slowmound mugo pine.

Composted soil, rich with microbes, was brought in from a local nursery for all the beds. All of the fruit and berry bushes produced in their first season and all the plants in this yard thrived! The trellis, arbor and patio furniture were made from sustainably-sourced local willow. This yard is not only fruitful and Earth-friendly, it is beautiful!

Annual, Biennial, Perennial

- *Perennial* – a flowering plant that blooms every year for a specific period. Some perennials bloom in the spring and again in the fall.

- *Annual* – a plant that sets seed and needs to be reseeded or planted every growing season. The flowers usually bloom all season long if you keep picking off the spent flowers (a practice called deadheading). Deadheading works because the plant must continue to flower to produce seeds.

- *Biennial* – a plant with a two-year growing cycle, which sets seed in the second year. It lives for two seasons. Usually biennials continue to reseed themselves, so a biennial patch can continue to grow on its own.

feature. But I laughed with surprise when I saw the desert section—a 21.5 sq. ft. square of cacti, sand and rocks, harboring the weathered backbone of a small animal—right near the public sidewalk!

GUIDELINES FOR CHOOSING PLANTS

Choose plants that will really thrive in the conditions of your yard—its ecosystem, plant zones, amount of sunlight. Plan for the long term and pick plants that will grow in the conditions that will likely be there in 10 to 50 years as the climate warms. For some areas, this means choosing plants that now grow in warmer zones. In other areas, such as the eastern slopes of the Rocky Mountains, it means planning for warmer, drier winters. Also, plan for the eventual size of the plant. In choosing your plants, remember to be a kind Gardener rather than a Warrior who pushes them to perform where they can't do well.

While an eco-yard would ideally contain native plants, having a selection of native and hardy plants may be what most suits your taste. Native cultivars can be very attractive and fill the same niche as native plants although they don't have as much attraction for pollinators. Choose plants that will grow in your ecosystem. If you live in the desert, choose plants suited to that ecosystem, which is dry and usually cool at night. If you want rainforest plants to grow in the desert, you need to have a sunroom or greenhouse!

Determine the plant zone classifications for your area and your yard, and choose plants that will grow in these zones. Plant zones are general indicators of where a plant will be hardy based on the average low temperature in that geographical region. You can find them on plant tags and in plant books and catalogs. Zone maps are available on the Internet and in plant books. You can get more specific information about suitable plants for your zone by checking with local garden centers, nurseries or horticultural societies. You can probably also find plant books specific to your area. Generally the higher numbers (Zone 7–8) will support plants that need lots of warmth. Zones 1 and 2 are for arctic-hardy plants. While zone maps will show your area's general zone, you may effectively have different zones in your yard and even in different parts of your yard, depending on its situation. For example, I lived for years in a Calgary neighborhood that is sheltered by an embracing, U-shaped escarpment. This neighborhood, Bridgeland, also contains many large trees that provide shelter from winds. The soil is fertile river silt. So while the rest of Calgary is shown as Zone 3 on plant maps, Bridgeland generally can support Zone 4 plants. In a really sheltered spot in your yard, you may be able to grow a plant that's rated one zone higher than the standard.

Plant zone classifications are a general guide, just one piece of information. Pam Wright of Bow Point Nursery calls Calgary "Zone X" because it really doesn't neatly fit into the zone system. The whole eastern slope regions of the Rocky Mountains in Canada and the U.S. are similar in that they generally have hot, dry days and cooler nights in the summer. Winters are cold, with occasional warm chinook winds that are tough on plants because they raise temperatures quickly and dry plants out, especially evergreens. Moreover, as our climate warms, some evergreen trees and birch trees are not as hardy in the chinook zone as they used to be. A few winters ago, many cedar trees in Alberta died, and Calgary nurseries will no longer guarantee them. I'm finding that juniper types need to be rated Zone 2 to cope with the drying chinooks and do well here now.

Native plant information and plants are probably available to you locally. Many new books on using native plants in landscaping are available. You can also refer to field guides to native plants for ideas. Native plant nurseries are burgeoning too. You may find some locally or be able to source native plants by mail order over the Internet. For example, three native plant nurseries serve the Calgary area. (See the Resources section at the end of the book.)

Match the sunlight requirements of the plants to the amount of sunlight in the spot in which you want to plant them. The sunlight requirements can be found on plant tags or in plant books. If a plant needs sun, that means six hours of direct sunlight per day during the growing season. You may need to monitor the sunlight in your yard to find out how much sun each area does get. If a plant is a shade plant, this means no direct sunlight. Again, be kind to your plants and site them appropriately. Note that most vegetables need sun, so site your vegetable garden in a sunny spot. Also site it where it will be sunny in years to come. My beloved grandfather planted three spruce trees south of his huge potato patch. Within ten years, the area got little direct sunlight, and the spruce trees sucked up most of the moisture—the area was no longer good for a vegetable garden. Forty years later, it is a totally dry shade garden.

Choose plants suited to the moisture available in the planting area. Plants are often categorized as growing well in shade or sun and moist or dry conditions. The trickiest places to plant are often the dry spots such as under the overhang of your roof. Be aware; people often forget that plants there will get no natural watering in the form of rain or snow. A low spot that tends to stay wet can also be tricky. A good plant book will have lists of suitable plants for different conditions of moisture and sunlight.

Choose plants suited to your soil conditions. This may be a little more challenging to determine and not always as critical as the factors noted above. Some plants are listed as needing lots of organic matter, so it's best not to plant them in clay or sandy soil. Plants that require lots of drainage are better in sandy and organically rich soils than in clay-rich soil. Some plants, like saskatoons or serviceberries, do best in clay soils without a lot of organic matter. Plants like juniper and blueberries thrive in sandy soils. Remember that your yard may not have uniform soil conditions and also that you can change soil conditions in a part of your yard to best suit the plants there. For example, you could refrain from adding compost to the soil near your saskatoon bush, which doesn't like too much organic matter. Some people have little desert plantings—this would be another place to refrain from adding compost and perhaps to add some sand. Further plantings could be planned to match the desert soil conditions. For plants that love organic matter, be sure to add compost to the soil when planting and to place compost on that soil on a regular basis.

Choose for the eventual size of the plant. Think long term—50 to 100 years ahead. How large will the plant be then? Read plant tags and books to find out how large the plant will grow and then allow it the space it needs. Books are generally more accurate, I find, than plant tags, which tend to underestimate the final size. Also ask local garden center and nursery staff how big the plant really grows, especially if it's a key tree in your design. Please respect your plants and plant them as a long-term legacy for future generations, rather than seeing them simply as outdoor decorations. And note that because of demand from those with newer, often smaller yards, nurseries are providing more columnar (thin) and dwarf (short) species. Ask about the eventual size of those species too—some grow just as big as regular trees, but more slowly!

Choose both male and female or just female trees and shrubs to provide balance to the ecosystem. Because so many homeowners are asking for trees that don't shed messy seedpods, nurseries are selling more male trees and shrubs than female ones. Thomas Ogren is an American horticulturalist who has a theory that this could be one reason for an increase in allergies in North America in the last decades.[2] Ask at the garden center or nursery for female trees. The staff may not know what you are talking about—recommend Ogren's books to them! (See Notes at the end of this chapter and the Resources section for details on Ogren's books.)

Choose plants you love! See your answers to the questions in the Clarify Your Aesthetics section earlier in this chapter to guide you. You will feel better and more connected to your yard if the plants are pleasing to you. I've had a few clients who've told me that they spent little time in their yards before I designed their gardens or added plants and beds. Now they love to be out in their yard. If there are plants now in your yard that you don't like, replace them with ones you love. One client didn't like to go out her back gate; she felt her crabapple was harassing her with its falling fruit. She also did not like the old honeysuckle that attracted neighborhood cats. She hadn't thought of replacing these trees; she felt she just had to live with them. I suggested she replace them, and we did—with trees she really enjoys. Now she feels much more comfortable and spends more time in her backyard.

Choose for color throughout the year. Plant a mix of plants that will provide color all year-long. In yards in my area of the world, I usually plant some evergreens to provide green during the winter. Planting trees and shrubs with colorful bark, such as red or yellow willows or red osier dogwood, can also add year-long color. Choosing perennials that bloom at different times will bring color throughout the growing season. In her book *Perennial Favorites*, Lois Hole offers a seasonal bar diagram to let you know when various perennials bloom, along with a list of plants sorted by color.

Plant smaller shrubs around deciduous trees (trees whose leaves fall off in winter in northern climes) to form a community around the tree and shelter it.[3]

Plant uneven numbers of plants. Many designers suggest that an uneven number (3, 5, 7) in same-plant groupings feels most natural. If you like even numbers, then do what feels right. A Chinese client of mine asks for plants to be planted in pairs for balance, as long as the numbers don't add up to 4, so I've planted three pairs of each plant in his beds.

Make It Easy on the Eyes

In placing perennials, consider the size (spread), the height, the color and the blooming period. Often, higher perennials are placed at the back of a bed with shorter perennials and annuals in front. Annuals provide much color and often have long blooming periods. As they need to be replanted every year, they do tend to be higher maintenance than perennials. I usually plant annuals to fill in the spaces between perennials, trees and shrubs until they reach their full size. I also plant annuals in hanging pots and deck containers. With all your plants, consider how the foliage and flowers will look when placed next to each other and consider complementary or contrasting foliage. For example, it's sometimes more pleasing to separate plants of different variegated foliages with those of plainer foliage.

SUMMARY

- Get clear on your intentions and preferences for your eco-yard before you design.
- Make sure your yardmates and neighbors are on side. Check municipal bylaws or ordinances to see if your design is legal.
- Use eco-yards and feng shui principles to guide your design.
- Choose plants appropriate to the conditions of your yard. Native and hardy plants are best for the local ecosystem.
- Design as if you were writing a piece of music—for melody, variation, harmony and flow.

NOTES

1. In Calgary, bylaws specify that lawn height must not exceed 6 in. (15 cm), yet this "shall not be interpreted to prevent the controlled and managed practice xeriscaping or other low water use gardening practices." So in an eco-yard that is managed, higher grass should be fine.

2. Thomas Ogren, *Safe Sex in the Garden and Other Propositions for an Allergy-free World* (Berkeley: Ten Speed Press, 2003), and *Allergy-free Gardening: The Revolutionary Guide to Healthy Landscaping* (Berkeley: Ten Speed Press, 2000).

3. Pam Wright, Bow Point Nurseries, Springbank, Alberta, makes this suggestion regarding planting shrubs around the base of trees to protect them.

11

Water-wise Design

Gardening requires a lot of water –
most of it in the form of perspiration.
—Lou Erickson

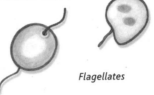

Flagellates

A key principle of eco-friendly landscaping is wise water use. Currently in the Western world, many of our water use practices are not sustainable. If current climate trends continue, gardeners can expect they'll have to reduce their use of treated water.

California provides a good example, and it's not unique—the state is an indicator of the water challenges that will be, or are currently being faced, elsewhere. Southern California has two sources of water, the Colorado River, which runs first through seven other thirsty states, and the San Joaquin–Sacramento River delta, or northern river delta, whose water comes from rain and snowfall in the northern mountains and enters the ocean in a wide series of canals near San Francisco. As mountain snowpacks diminish and other water-hungry pressures on the Colorado River increase (including crop irrigation in a state that grows large quantities of food), less water is available to Southern California from these sources. The northern river delta must also supply Northern California. As sea levels rise (due to global warming), it's increasingly challenging to protect the fresh delta water from becoming salty with sea water. On top of this, shipping this water around the state uses 20 percent of California's energy.

People in Southern California are looking at alternatives—for example, a desalinization plant that can turn sea water into fresh water. But desalinization takes a tremendous amount of energy. The pilot project will use non-renewable petroleum, creating pollution and greenhouse gases. Fifty percent of the treated water in Southern California is used to water lawns and yards—in a desert ecosystem! This makes no sense, and municipal officials in Southern California are encouraging landscaping more suited to the ecosystem.

Water experts say a wide range of solutions will be needed to meet the water challenge, including

• homeowner water conservation
• restricting or banning use of treated water on landscapes
• separating drinking water systems from other uses. For example, landscaping water could come from untreated sources, greywater (household drain water from sinks and tubs) or treated sewer water.

In your eco-yard, you can design, construct and plant in ways that use our precious water most wisely and help restore water resources. Water-wise landscape designs include

• rain and snowmelt water capture-and-use systems that take care of water needs onsite
• landscape features, such as beds or naturalized plantings, that maximize the amount of water that will soak into the soil of your yard. This water will percolate down through the ground to replenish underground water aquifers.
• minimization of watering needs
• selection of plants that require little water

RAIN BARRELS

One easy way to capture water that falls onto your roof is in rain barrels. You could have these at every downspout and could also have a series of barrels that pour into each other. Rain barrels are pretty easy to come by these days. Packaging companies that sell used 50-gallon (190-liter) plastic drums are an inexpensive source. (Try to find barrels that have not been used for chemicals.) I use barrels that have been used to ship apple juice concentrate. Often, the supplier will put a little tap near the bottom. I find it handy to have the top sawn off to act as a lid, so I can just dunk my watering cans into the barrel. This fills them much more quickly than the tap

Fixing Leaky Hose Connections

If your hoses start leaking around the attachments, it's probably because they need a new washer or because the brass end of the hose has bent—usually from being dropped on the ground. Try putting in a new washer on the hose end first. If this does not work, buy new brass ends and clamps at the hardware store, cut the hose ends off and clamp on the new ends.

will. And a lid is also good to prevent insects like mosquitoes from breeding in the open, standing water.

A variety of downspout diverters can be purchased at garden centers or greenhouse supply stores that will take the water from your downspout into the rain barrel and channel any overflow into the downspout. With an extension, the downspout can then be directed away from your house foundation to an area of your yard that needs water.

istockphoto.com/Igor Kisselev

Oak rain barrel

It's also possible to purchase large plastic rain barrels that can hold up to 93 gallons (350 liters) of water.

Oak barrels that have been used for making whiskey make attractive rain barrels. They do require a bit of tending (keeping the wood wet from the top if they are empty). You can often purchase these from distillers or at garden centers.

When it comes to watering using your rain barrels, you can use watering cans. You could also hook a hose to the rain barrel tap and then attach it to a soaker hose placed where you want to water. The pressure is often quite low in rain barrels that sit on the ground, so this latter method takes a while. It helps to raise the barrel to create higher water pressure. To use the tap on most rain barrels, you have to raise them a little anyway. The rounded concrete bricks used to make firepits work well for this. You could also build a platform. If you want to use the "dunk from the top" method when the barrel is on a platform, you will likely need to build a step to climb up on.

Sloping for Drainage

If you are doing your own landscaping, remember to slope the land so that water will run away from your house. If you are doing major changes or new landscaping, consider the water drainage near the house and around the site. Design so that water will be most wisely used in your yard—normally to water the plants.

CISTERNS

Depending on your climate and conditions, you may be able to install a large underground tank to hold your rainwater. You would then use a pump to water when needed. I've heard of people placing these under decks or patios, excavating for the cistern before building the deck or patio.

FRENCH DRAINS

If you don't want to bother with rain barrels, you can create a system in which the water runs from your downspout under the ground to soak the soil from below. You would have to excavate to create this system. If you are excavating your yard anyway (say, you are replacing your lawn with beds!), this could be an ideal time to install a French drain.

To build a French drain, you dig a trench on a slight slope (see What Is a Slight Slope later in this chapter) out into your yard, ending in a well that can be filled with river rock. Place a few inches or centimeters of

Weeping tile with a sock in a French drain trench. The well at the end will be filled with grapefruit-sized river rocks. The pipe will be covered with gravel, then soil, and the area planted.

gravel along the bottom and sides of this trench—usually road crush mix is least expensive and works well. From the end of your downspout, install pipe (usually plastic PVC pipe) that connects to an elbow and another section of solid pipe running out into your yard. At the point in your yard where you want water to seep, you hook up 4 in. (10 cm) drainage pipe (with holes in it, wrapped in landscape fabric or a sleeve of cloth, to keep dirt from clogging up the holes). This type of pipe is also called weeping tile and the cover is called a sock. This drainage pipe lies on the gravel in the trench and ends at your well of rock. Then cover the drainage pipe with a 4 in. (10 cm) layer of gravel. Once the gravel and pipes are installed, lay quality soil on top of them and put plants in.

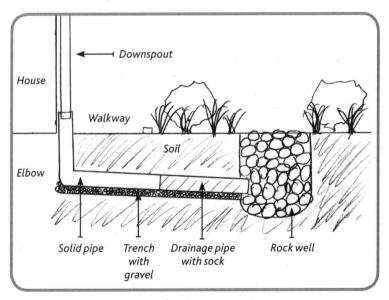

French drain – side view

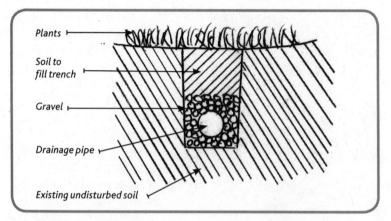

French drain – cross-section

This is how a French drain works: Rainwater runs into the pipes and drains into the soil from the holes in the drainage pipe. If the rain is heavy, the water can pool in the well of river rock and flow over gently into the yard. (The well would usually be in the middle of a bed.) It's important that your underground trench is sloped toward the yard and away from the house foundation. Ensure the trench is deep enough that the pipe is below the frost line (the depth to which the ground freezes in winter[1]). Otherwise it could shift with frost heave. Call a local builder or building supply store to learn where the frost line is in your area.

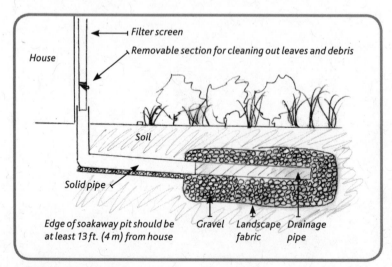

Soakaway pit – side view

What Is a Slight Slope?

Use a level when you are creating a slope for water runoff. You are looking for a two-percent slope or slightly more. Set the level in along the entire bottom of your trench to make sure the slope is continuous. The little bubble in the level should just touch the upward edge of the line marker.

A variation of this method is the soakaway pit. Dig a trench as you would for a French drain and also dig a big hole at the end of it. Place a large piece of landscape fabric in the bottom of the hole, large enough to wrap all around the gravel. Fill the bottom of the trench and the hole with gravel. Run solid pipe to the hole and place drainage pipe in the hole. Cover the pipe with a thin layer of gravel, fill the hole with gravel and wrap the landscape fabric around the gravel. Then fill the trench and cover the hole with soil and plant. A soakaway pit allows water to soak into the ground. As with a French drain, make sure the trench and pipe are below frost level. Ensure too that your gravel pit is large enough to handle the runoff. If you want to build a soakaway pit, I suggest you do some more research.[2] I prefer the French drain as extra runoff has a place to go!

USE WALKWAYS TO SPREAD WATER

Proponents of permaculture offer this idea for water conservation: Have water flow into level walkways set against beds. This spreads the water evenly to the beds. So if you replace your lawn with beds, you could have the downspout from the roof run away from the house foundation into a walkway created from digging out or covering over sod. Just make sure the water cannot drain back against the house foundation (a matter of distance and slope away from the house). If you use this walkway in a winter climate, make sure you can divert water elsewhere in winter to prevent a skating rink!

Cover the walkway with a thick (1 in. or 3 cm) layer of newspaper or cardboard and then 3 in. (8 cm) of pea gravel or rounded rock. The pea gravel will be easy on your feet and will allow water to flow through without creating mud.

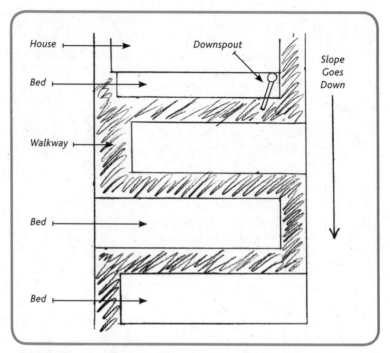

Joined walkways spread water on a slope

If your yard is on a slope, you could create walkways running perpendicular to the slope, joined with little water runways on the ends that run down the slope to spread the water all through your beds.

ROCK RIVERS

Another way to channel water attractively through your yard is to build a rock river from your downspout area out into your yard. Just dig a trench and fill it with rock. Again, be sure the water will not

This rock river was built to drain water from beside the house to beds in the front yard. First a trench sloped to the front yard was dug and filled with road crush gravel mix.

Different-sized local rocks (from construction sites and other homeowners) were then placed to look like a natural stream.

drain back against the house foundation. The river needs to start a little ways away from the house and have a slight downward slope. For the most natural look, use river rock or rounded, weathered rock that might be naturally found in a river or stream. Use a variety of boulders and different sizes of rock too. Think about an appropriate location for the end of your river so that any water that runs right to the end drains properly.

For example, the heather-inspired yard I mentioned in Chapter 10, Designing Your Eco-yard, featured a rock river that ran from the downspout at a corner of the house to a rock pool by a sandstone ledge we built about six feet (two meters) short of the city sidewalk to prevent runoff onto the sidewalk. The homeowner loved pink-colored granite, and I was able to obtain some granite boulders for his river. Most of the other rocks (also pink and grey) were split river rocks used in a sweat lodge. For a natural filled-in look for the little river, I used 1.25 in. (3 cm) Montana river rock that comes in beautiful purple, teal and pink tones. This river looks stunning when wet. See the color pages for photos.

A BOG GARDEN OR TRENCH

Rock rivers may be most appropriate in dry regions. If you live in an area that can support water-loving plants, you could plant them along the edges of your rock river, or simply plant water-loving plants in a trench that runs from your downspout. The trench could end in a bog area in which you plant bog-loving plants. These are the plants that would grow along streams and rivers, or in swamps or sloughs, in your native ecosystem.

Watch Your Indicator Plants

I have a Ligularia plant that I love. It has large elephant-ear-shaped leaves and spiky yellow flowers that bloom for at least a month in late summer. It needs watering at least once a week in the heat of summer. When my Ligularia gets droopy, that's my signal to check on my other water-lovers too.

GROUP WATER-LOVING PLANTS

In the chapter on design, I suggested choosing plants that are hardy for the temperature and moisture conditions of your site, so they will need little or no watering once established (one or two years). If you have some plants you love that will need extra watering, group them together in plantings to which you can run a water system (end of drainspout, a French drain, possibly a rock river or plant trench). You could also plant them in a spot handy to your rain barrels, from which you can simply use your watering can. If you really need to turn on the hose, you will use less water if the thirstiest plants are grouped together.

DRIP IRRIGATION SYSTEMS

Drip irrigation systems sport little pipes above ground with holes that drip water exactly where the plant needs it. These can be very useful in vegetable gardens and greenhouses and can usually be purchased through greenhouse suppliers. You configure the system to fit your plantings.

IRRIGATION SYSTEMS

Underground residential irrigation systems that turn on regularly to water your yard are not so water-wise or generally good for your plants. They tend to water the leaves rather than the soil and roots. This can lead to fungal problems on your plant leaves. They also don't necessarily water when your plants need it. Arborists have told me that many of the problems associated with residential trees stem from overwatering by irrigation systems.

These systems are also difficult to maintain. They often leak underground, which goes unnoticed, wastes water and can kill your plants with overwatering.

SOAKER HOSES

One option for easy watering of planted beds is to place soaker hoses under your mulch. This will get the water into the soil near the plant roots. Soaker hoses are made from rubber or plastic, and through tiny holes, they release water all along the length of the hose. They usually come in 25- and 50-foot (10- and 20-meter) lengths and can be found at hardware stores and garden centers. Wind the soaker hose through your bed so it will leak water at the drip line of each plant (where rain would drip from the outside plant leaves). When you want to water, just attach a regular hose to the end of the soaker hose and turn the water on low pressure. Leave the water on for a few hours. You could attach a hose from one of your rain barrels for this purpose. When plants are newly planted and getting established, soaking them for three hours once a week for the first six weeks or so is normally required. Then you can taper off the watering, and by the second or third year, your hardy plants will no longer need watering.

You can attach soaker hoses to each other to make them longer, but beyond 100 feet (40 meters) of length your water pressure will usually be too low to reach the end. One option is to use a hose splitter so that you can attach your garden hose to two separate soaker hoses at once.

SUMMARY

• Sustainable landscaping uses little, if any, treated water.
• Design your yard so that snowmelt or rain that falls on your yard is used to water your plants and/or to soak into your soil to replenish underground aquifers.
• Use mostly plants that need little extra watering and group those that do need extra watering.

NOTES

1. The frost line is said to be from 1.5 to 4 ft. or 60 to 160 cm in Calgary. Just west of Calgary, the M.D. of Rocky View considers the frost line to be 4 ft. or 160 cm. It is best to check with a local builder or building supply store.

2. Daniel Lefebvre and Susan Fisher, *Landscape Guide for Canadian Homes* (Ottawa: Canada Mortgage and Housing Corporation, 2004). This guide has more detailed information on water-wise landscape construction including more information on soakaway pits.

12

Growing Vegetables in the Eco-yard (by Caron Wenzel)

*Earth here is so kind, that just tickle her with a hoe
and she laughs with a harvest .*
—*Douglas William Jerrold*

Bacteria

Few things in life are as rewarding as when, on your walk through a vegetable garden, you pick a fresh herb or vegetable and smell that indescribable earthy burst, then savor the piquant flavor of homegrown food. Indeed, the whole experience is a total immersion in the realm of natural sensation. The bright warm sun, buzzing insects and fragrant aromas, the many hues of green and the vegetables themselves can engage us in a way few other things can.

People grow food for many reasons. Of course, there is the practical need to eat, but vegetable gardening confers many other benefits too. It can allow us to express and maintain our ties to the past by

> Off over yonder,
> Toward the North-land,
> Will it prove that my yellow corn grains
> Shall grow and bear fruit, asking which I now sing.
> –Zuni planting song

growing Grandma's favorite green beans or cucumbers. Herbs can evoke a memory of a shared holiday dish that requires a homegrown component from the fall harvest. Cultivation is vital for physical survival and, in a wider sense, essential to our human experience.

The vegetable gardening season actually starts in the winter right after New Year's with the arrival of the seed catalogs. Sitting before a cozy fire with the page open to pictures of the coming summer's squash or pumpkins is the stuff of dreams. Trying new kinds of vegetables with an eye to capturing a desirable flavor or pinpointing a variety that can survive and prosper in one's local climate is truly the fun of gardening.

Vegetables are different from other plants because they require human intervention to actually get them to grow. "Plant people" the world over are good at growing many species—trees, shrubs, perennials—but the legendary tales of "green thumbs" are told about vegetable gardeners. In fact, people have competitions all over for bragging rights to the largest pumpkins, the biggest cabbage, most flavorful tomato or whatever grows in the region. Onion festivals, garlic festivals, chili pepper festivals—all have reason to celebrate. So, how to get in on the action?

STARTING AN ORGANIC GARDEN

Before you set out into the yard with seed packets and shovel, you need a plan and a plot, kind of like writing a book! Pick a spot in the yard, anywhere with full sun for six or more hours per day. This is absolutely essential. Annual vegetables are sun worshippers. Soil for vegetables is actually optional, but sun isn't. Which brings us to some general rules when planting a garden:

Location, location, location. Some leaf and root vegetables can get by on four to six hours a day of direct sun. But many vegetables require at least six hours of sun a day. They will not grow in the shade. More than six hours is ideal. Fewer than six hours, for heat lovers like tomatoes, will cause them to grow leaves profusely but not set fruit.

Most vegetables are annual or biennial. An annual is a plant that grows and sets seed yearly. A biennial has a two-year growing cycle and sets seed in the second year. A perennial is a plant that returns every year and can live to be quite old. Some perennial vegetables are rhubarb, asparagus, horseradish, alliums (onion family) and Jerusalem artichoke.

The temperature must be above freezing for vegetables to grow without protection.

If a human likes to eat something, so does the neighborhood wildlife. To protect it from plant browsers like deer and rabbits, a vegetable garden may need some type of fence or enclosure. A fenced-in garden with rabbit wire at the base of the fencing will discourage most nibblers. In heavy deer areas, 10 ft. (3 m) light fencing may be necessary. Many gardeners have favorite tricks to repel pesky critters, such as garlic and pepper sprays, fox urine, fish emulsion fertilizer (doing double duty), moving reflective strips or plastic owls. Experimentation and experience will show what works best.

A PERSONAL GARDEN STYLE

An eco-yard is very personal because it is where one lives, works, relaxes, grows food and appreciates the beauty of nature. It is a pathway to co-creation with the plants, insects and animals of a particular bioregion. My own garden and eco-yard is a 20-year adventure into my own little bit of the natural world. It is my teacher and living laboratory.

My starting point was a natural yard using native plants specific to the bioregion around Chicago. This practice, called restoration ecology, involves replacing resource-intensive lawns and plants not adapted to a local area with natives and native plant gardens. The goal is to retain water and return it to local aquifers, prevent erosion and minimize the need for water through drought conditions. My native yard functions as described, but I wanted it all: a heirloom vegetable garden, herbs, good soil, plants I had fond memories of from childhood and a place for my grandmother's heirloom rhubarb.

My yard today comprises native prairie, woodland and wetland plots, an organic vegetable garden, an herb garden and a food forest. A food

198 | ECO-YARDS: SIMPLE STEPS TO EARTH-FRIENDLY LANDSCAPES

forest is made up of perennial plants that can be used for food, fiber, building material or medicine, configured in imitation of a forest so that it makes the most use of the land. It's a *permaculture*-designed eco-yard that includes elements of all the other garden types described below. In my yard are elements of the *square foot* garden for carrots, beets and cucumbers; the *lasagna* garden method to build the soil and start new garden beds; *deep-dug* intensive beds for poor soil areas that need more than just a topdressing of compost and finally the *three sisters* method to keep weeds in check. These methods are described below, as are a couple of types of vegetable beds you can create.

TYPES OF VEGETABLE BEDS AND GROWING METHODS

Raised beds

A 4 ft. by 4 ft. (1.5 m by 1.5 m) square area is an ideal size for a raised bed, as the vegetables can be reached from both sides of the bed. It is easy to enclose an area with cedar, scrap lumber, boards (see comments below) or fence posts laid horizontally on the ground in a sunny area. Stone and concrete block will also work, but in the case of concrete, the bed may require more watering, as concrete tends to absorb water. If your sunny area is in the front yard, don't worry— decorative fencing and flowerbeds around the perimeter of the garden are an opportunity to be an eco-gardener. Fill with topsoil, compost and other soil amendments (see Lasagna gardening below). The soil in a raised bed can be 6 to 24 in. (15 to 60 cm) deep. A raised bed can also be placed in unexpected places such as on a patio or roof, for urban gardeners. Raised beds can be placed in a series. Some people like a seating platform around the perimeter to allow for comfortable seated gardening.

Lumber that is sustainably sourced, such as beetle-killed timber, is a good material to use for garden beds. Don't use old rail ties or treated lumber of any kind because these contain chemicals. Even small amounts of these chemicals are poisonous and carcinogenic. Treated lumber contains arsenic, which can be absorbed by the garden vegetables.

Raised row beds

A more traditional approach to gardening is to plant in rows within a garden area. People with large sunny yards can install this type of garden. A row can be as long as the gardener chooses. An advantage of this configuration is easy access to the plants for watering and weeding; the disadvantage is it takes up a lot of space relative to a more intensive-style garden. Mulching the rows heavily insures the retention of moisture and suppression of weeds (see Chapter 7, Making Beds to Replace Your Lawn).

Growing methods

Gardening is as easy as A, B, C (and D and E). The gardening methods listed below are the ones I have found most useful. And in truth, my design style is a combination of all five.

A. *Permaculture* is a whole system of gardening, landscaping and native plantings whose purpose is harmony with a discrete local area. Australian agronomist Bill Mollison devised this design method in the 1970s when he became disenchanted with conventional agricultural practices. It has become a modern model for sustainable living and gardening.

B. *Square foot gardening* is a method developed by Mel Bartholomew that allows the home gardener to get high yields from common garden vegetables in small spaces. A 4 ft. (1.5 m) square area can yield 32 carrots, 12 bunches of lettuce, 18 bunches of spinach, 16 radishes, 16 scallions, 16 beets, 9 Japanese turnips, 5 pounds peas, 1 head of cabbage, 4 heads of romaine lettuce, 1 head of cauliflower, and 1 head of broccoli! He relies on compost and good soil care.

C. *Double-dug bio-intensive* is actually a method developed by the French and expanded on by the noted American organic gardener John Jeavons, who advocates really building the soil up with humus, compost and other organic soil amendments, at high quantities. In the 19th century, millions of Parisians ate courtesy of deeply dug raised garden beds to which had been added tons of horse manure—easily available from the city's streets and stables. This method, which restores the bio-zoo of soil micro-organisms, is very effective in areas with little soil, no soil or very depleted soil.

D. *Three sisters gardening* (corn, squash, beans and sunflowers) is based on an understanding that plants do better when they live together with their "friends." Native Americans realized that biodiversity was very important. Also known as intercropping, this method allows for many types of plants to be grown in a given area. Because the soil is kept covered throughout the growing season, weeds are suppressed.

E. Lasagna gardening is a favorite of mine. A no-till, layered, raised-bed garden (that needs a very sunny spot), the lasagna garden is the easiest to create. No-till has the advantages of being back-friendly, reducing or eliminating weeds and allowing you to garden in unusual places. There's no need to dig, just layer. Layering is a natural process that builds organic plant material over time, composting itself, allowing plants to grow in areas where the soil is poor or nonexistent.

See the Resources section for books on these different methods.

Building the lasagna garden

Collect newspaper, cardboard, well-seasoned compost, straw, grass clippings and well-rotted herbivore manure (cow, horse, sheep) and begin the layering process. Your best friends are a good wheelbarrow and a pitchfork.

1. Mark off a 4 ft. by 4 ft. (1.25 m by 1.25 m) square bed in your sunny area.

2. Surround the bed with untreated timbers or fieldstone in the above configuration to a height of about 4 to 8 in. (10 to 20 cm).

3. Lay down at least 15 sheets of newspaper (roughly half a newspaper; a full newspaper is better) or one layer of cardboard (whatever is most available). Overlap the edges by at least 6 in. (15 cm).

4. Next, place a layer of well-rotted manure.

5. Follow with old straw, leaves or grass clippings or a mixture of all three to a depth of 3 to 4 in. (7.5 to 10 cm).

6. Continue layering the rotted herbivore manure with the leaves, straw and grass clippings until the bed is about 8 in. (20 cm) tall.

Finish with a 1 in. (2.5 cm) layer of wood ash from a campfire or fireplace. (Please, for health's sake, no burned garbage!) Follow with a mulching top layer of good clean wood chips to suppress weed germination.

7. Water well to start the compost process.

Peat Moss in the Lasagna—or Not?

Some books recommend peat moss as an ingredient for a lasagna or intensive garden. Mined from peat bogs throughout the world, peat moss is a limited resource and not considered renewable. An acceptable replacement in planting mixtures is coconut shell coir, a by-product of coconut growing, but often shipped long distances. This is an optional ingredient.

The ratio overall should be four parts brown material (compost, leaves, wood chips) to one part green and high-nitrogen material (grass clippings, vegetable scraps, rotted manure). You can then let the lasagna "cook" for six weeks or over the winter. Or you can plant immediately using vegetable starts. To plant started vegetables or seed, just open a space in the layers, fill with compost or topsoil and plant the seedling. To seed directly into the row, dig an 3 in. (8 cm) "V" trench in the layered bed, fill with compost or topsoil and plant normally.

These beds can be built up year after year as the previous year's layers break down. No digging, and this method will rebuild soil too! Lasagna gardening is also a great way to build habitat for micro-organisms and

Beds Need Rest Too

Lasagna Gardening author Patricia Lanza uses both "rested" and "unrested" beds, but prefers fall-prepared beds for spring planting. A "rested" bed is an area of layered materials that has been allowed to break down, forming humus and losing volume in the process.

the decomposers, greatly improving soil health. Feed the soil and the plants will be fed. Spraying these beds with actively aerated compost teas will add even more nutrients and microbes and make them available to the plants.

Vegetable garden tidbits

Once you have an established garden, remember to rotate beds of staple vegetables such as cabbage family and tomato family members each year. Planting vegetables in the same place year after year is an open invitation to fungal, bacterial and pest-borne diseases. Companion planting is also very important for many reasons: many herbs and flowers contain oils that repel insects. Planting multiple types of flowers and herbs throughout the garden, in and among the vegetables, will protect the vegetables from harmful insects and attract beneficial ladybugs, lacewings and mantises. Flowers and herbs will also attract pollinators to the garden in areas of low biodiversity.

Unconventional configurations in gardens

Vegetables make great garden plantings anywhere around a house or eco-yard. These days gardeners are mixing vegetables into flower beds and vice versa with wonderful results. Some of the most productive yards food-wise don't even look like vegetable gardens. They are configured to be multi-purpose. A layered (lasagna) bed can be put in the front yard, for example, surrounded by edible flowers and planted with herbs, lettuces and spinach, perhaps located near fruit trees. The layered bed has thus become a beautiful food producer in the eco-yard. Circular configurations of layered beds can hold more plants of varying heights. These are especially useful for herb gardens.

SUMMARY

Growing one's own food is more than just being a gardener. Those of us who maintain vegetable gardens learn many things. One is that gardening will feed a person well but also teaches humility. Getting that perfect carrot or lettuce can sometimes be a challenge.

Here are some key points to remember in organic vegetable gardening:

• Build layered garden beds.
• Rotate crops from year to year.
• Companion plant.
• Be creative.

Remember, the tastiest, most healthful eco-friendly food comes from your own yard, year after year!

Overview

*There is no more strong statement of
faith in the future than planting a tree.*
—Thornton Wilder

Why take the eco-yards approach? Simply, **to restore balance and
health to the local, regional and global ecosystem**. We can landscape
in ways that restore natural ecosystems. At the least, we can take steps
to stop harmful practices—such as using pesticides, synthetic fertilizers,
power machinery and excessive water.

The good news is that **landscaping this way takes less money and
labor in the long run**, even though it may take some investment at
first. It also feels really good to know you're participating in working
for a healthy future for the Earth.

How? The first step is to embrace the Gardener archetype: understand
how you and your yard are part of the large web of interaction among
all life on Earth and **work with the natural ecosystem rather than
fighting or trying to control it**. This may take some shifts in attitude
and some learning at first. The good news again—this way of doing
things can be less work and more fulfilling in the long term than
gardening like a Warrior.

**Design your yard with a wide diversity of plants that are hardy
in your local ecosystem**. Hardy plants should need little care (e.g.,
watering). Plants native to your region (they grow in the wild) best
support the local ecosystem because they provide food to native
pollinators and habitat for local wildlife.

Minimize lawn areas to where you use them or where they are the most practical choice (e.g., a firebreak around a rural home). Why? Lawns generally don't meet the criteria for an eco-yard: diverse, hardy and locally native. Generally made up of a single species, lawns tend to take the most care of any yard feature. **Where you do want lawn, change the grass types over to hardy, low-maintenance varieties.** This can be done by overseeding other grasses into your current lawn for a few years.

Replacing your lawn does not have to mean a lot of excavating or digging. **You can cover-over your lawn with newspaper, soil and mulch.** You can even build the soil as you go by layering grass clippings, leaves and kitchen scraps.

Use compost to restore organic matter to your soil. Compost provides the best food for your plants. It also **restores the all important soil micro-organisms.** These soil micro-organisms are critical to life on Earth. They break down organic matter and work with plants to bring them the food they need to grow. Without microbes, plants don't grow. Without plants, animals don't live.

So microbes are important, and they could use some help. Chemical pesticide and fertilizer use and lots of tilling of the Earth have reduced microbe numbers in the Earth's soil over the last century. The good news? Microbes come back quickly with compost and good conditions. Actively aerated compost tea made with good compost is an inexpensive way to restore microbes. **Using compost and compost tea is a good road to health for your yard.**

Growing food in your yard is a way to lessen your dependence on the industrial food system, which, in producing most of our food in the Western world, has a pretty big impact on the environment—including the widespread use of harmful chemicals, single-crop cultivation over large areas and the pollution and non-renewable resource use associated with transporting food over long distances. So **growing your own food is another way you can help restore the global ecosystem.** And your own food is usually the tastiest, healthiest food you'll ever eat.

Take it further. You can take the things you do in your own yard out into the community too! **Join in or support community gardens—**

unused municipal land or private land where community members come together to grow food, each participant tending his or her own plot. Community gardens have been great success stories in rebuilding community spirit in many locales. Even if you don't participate in one, let your politicians know that you support this use of land. Your local community garden may need a donation too.

Take some initiative on the political level. It can only take a few minutes to make a phone call or send an email to let your politicians know you want them to support measures to restore the ecosystem. Such measures include

• laws that phase out unnecessary pesticide use
• naturalizing public spaces—growing hardy native plants in these areas
• support for farmers' markets, where locally grown food and products are sold
• retaining land near urban centers for food production

Thank your politicians for any work they have done in supporting such initiatives.

This is all life-affirming work. Enjoy it! Have fun bringing more beauty and health into the world!

Afterword

The highest reward for a person's toil is not what
they get from it but who they become through it.
—John Ruskin

I came to write this book through a health crisis that helped
me deeply learn how we are all interconnected and that our
choices and actions do affect other beings. I am now almost
fully recovered from sensitivities to chemicals that came on
after a home renovation a few years ago.

Landscaping provided a healing avenue to focus my mind and energy
on life and beauty as I recovered. A 15-year hobby turned into a
business. And when I found myself needing to leave my neighborhood
for a few days whenever neighbors used pesticides (or the lawn spray
companies came by), I got involved in the movement to enact laws to
phase out cosmetic pesticide use. Suddenly this was important enough
for me to act.

I learned that most people want to use natural landscaping methods
once they know why this is so important—they just don't know *how*
to do it. So I started teaching and writing about how to landscape
naturally. Out of that came this book.

Along the way, I went to a talk about actively aerated compost tea.
At the time, I was feeling despair about the state of the planet and
hopeless to act when I was so ill. Learning about compost tea gave
me a lifeline of hope and brought me out of that despair. Doing my
part to help restore soil micro-organisms was a positive action I could
take that would make a difference. I took classes, researched, spoke
to landscapers and organic experts across North America, and had

equipment made for spraying compost tea. I worked to figure out how to translate the success compost tea had in agriculture to an urban landscape setting, grateful for my early background in science and love of biology! I started offering my Eco-yards Spray Service for Calgary yards in 2007.

In 2008 my landscaping business blossomed after I installed a display garden at the Calgary Horticultural Society Garden Show. The display garden featured an edible, sustainable yard with wood chip–covered flower beds, apple trees, raspberry and currant bushes, raised vegetable beds, a small hardy grass lawn and log slice pathways. People *really* responded to the Eco-yards approach!

I offer design, installation and the Eco-yards Spray Service in Calgary, Alberta, Canada. For more information, or to hire my company, contact me at 403-969-1176, info@eco-yards.com or eco-yards.com.

I intend to keep writing and sharing on how to landscape the eco-yards way. As I and colleagues around the globe pioneer new ways, or rework old ways, to farm, garden and landscape in harmony with the planet, we're constantly learning. So please help me learn and share. If you have feedback on this book, stories to share or avenues to support spreading the eco-yards way, I'd love to hear from you at info@ eco-yards.com.

Tauveen Lame

P.S. Acting to create a healthier, more beautiful world is keeping me hopeful. I hope this book encourages you to act too.

Acknowledgments

This book came about through the support and encouragement of many people. I am grateful to them all, including the many not mentioned below. The support of my parents, Bill and Marg Rama, was instrumental. They sheltered me in my recovery from illness and continued to support me as I wrote. They both were sounding boards for my ideas and initial readers for much of the book. My love of nature was instilled by them through our many outdoor adventures when I was young. Their zeal and creativity in renovating every yard they moved to (many!) served as a great apprenticeship. Their knowledge of science and the way they brought it to everyday life (my father a chemical engineer and my mother a nurse) gave me an appreciation for understanding how the world works.

Cindy Tuer was the first to suggest that I write this book. Her belief in me was the seed. Kathleen Mailer nourished that seed, inspiring me to start. Karen Morrison was instrumental in my taking a compost tea spraying service to urban customers. She enthusiastically provided the avenues for me to teach about microbes to school children and master composters. Through Karen I realized how important and fun it was to help people learn about microbes.

My landscaping and design clients pushed my learning with their questions, insistence on eco-friendly ways, and the opportunity to work in their yards. My landscaping crews over the years helped me refine techniques, worked hard and made it a fun adventure.

Matthew George, Joe Whaley, Ted Leischner, Tim Livingstone, Jerome Osentowski, Becky Elder, John Cowan, Bruce Tainio, Jesse Lemieux, Pam and Ken Wright, Steve Repic and Barb Kinnie have been greatteachers for me about compost tea and sustainable urban landscaping.

Deborah Flynn took most of the fabulous photographs in this book. Joan Caplan took the author photograph. Photos of many Calgarians' gardens are here including that of Joey Stewart and Ken and Lynn Martin. Marichu Antonio, Brian Gallagher, and Soil Foodweb, Inc. graciously shared their photos. Deborah Barney and Daniel Ruesch caught the importance of making microbes real for people and paid tremendous attention to learning about microbes and illustrating them.

Thank you to those who contributed to the first edition of Eco-yards: Kyle Loranger Design, Daniel Ruesch, Gerald Wheatley, Lynn Russell, Nance Kuenz, Sandra Holy, Tim Livingstone, Matthew and Christine George, Kelly O'Gorman, Pam and Ken Wright, Patsy Price, Joan Caplan, Karen Braun, and Jacqueline Puff.

Judy Millar's thoughtfulness, friendliness, intelligence and love of the Earth make her the perfect editor for this book. She challenged me to know what I was writing about. She made the thoughts clearer and more accessible to others. Patsy Price's masterful editing hand is also in here.

Caron Wenzel wrote initial drafts of the compost and vegetables chapters and when I was stuck, she generously shared her knowledge and perspective, helping me to clarify the basic concepts. Her spirit and enthusiasm shine through in this book.

Thank you to the New Society Publishers team for lovingly taking this creation to a broader audience.

The inspiration and support of my teachers over the years has been critical in allowing me to write this book. Armand Huet DeGrenier led me through my early shamanic years and encouraged me to follow my vision. I am deeply grateful to The Way of the Heart teachers: Kimberly Herkert, Daniel Goodenough and Eduardo Parra. Kimberly provides such an inspiring role model of creative visioning, positive language, hope and beauty. Daniel has supported me and countless others in following our life mission. Eduardo has been a good and truthful friend. The Way of the Heart community has been instrumental in this book. Check them out at www.thewayoftheheart.com.

Thank you to all those who bought copies of the first edition (on spec) before it was complete. Your belief in the value of this work kept me going to complete it.

Resources

Gardening is popular and resources abound! These are resources I have found useful. Some of these resources are specific to Alberta, Canada, and the Northern Great Plains of North America. Future Eco-yards offerings may include resources for more regions. Check eco-yards.com to stay informed.

CHAPTER 1 – THE GARDENER

Many great thinkers have written about the topic of restoring a healthy relationship between humans and the rest of the natural world. If you want to explore more, try these resources:

• Any writing by Wendell Berry.
• *The Dream of the Earth* by Thomas Berry.
• *Nature and the Human Soul* by Bill Plotkin.
• *World As Lover, World As Self* by Joanna Macy.
• Matthew Fox, a "green" Christian, has written many books.
• Hildegard von Bingen wrote poetry and music and painted in medieval times.

CHAPTER 2 – WHAT IS AN ECO-YARD?

• invasive.org details invasive species for North America including weeds, bugs, diseases and others. The website also has a good selection of links on the home page.
• Michael Pollan has written books and articles, and been featured on Web videos and radio about eco-gardening in the broadest sense. His books include *The Botany of Desire, The Omnivore's Dilemma* and *In Defense of Food*. He has the most entertaining and understandable

analysis of the industrial food system's effect on our health and the environment that I have come across. Along the way, he explains how we got into chemical agriculture (and landscaping) and also how organic agriculture has evolved. In *The Omnivore's Dilemma*, he profiles Joel Salatin's Polyface Farm in Virginia, U.S.A., as a shining example of how we can raise food in a humane way that leaves the Earth healthier than we found it.

• Arborist-cut wood chips, log slices, rustic logs and furniture are available at Bow Point Nursery near Calgary in Springbank, Alberta. bowpointnursery.com. Tel: 403-686-4434.

CHAPTER 3 – WHY ECO-YARDS?

• A video by the Canadian Association of Physicians for the Environment (CAPE), "Lawn Pesticides: Reducing Harm", is a quick overview of why and how to go organic in your yard. To view the video, follow the link from healthycalgary.ca/Page-3.html. The video can also be purchased from CAPE in Toronto, Ontario, Canada (416-306-2273).

• beyondpesticides.org and panna.org are U.S. websites with comprehensive information about pesticides and alternatives.

• eco-yards.com, my website, has links to articles on the health effects of pesticides and why government pesticide regulations are inadequate.

CHAPTER 4 – ECO-MAINTENANCE

• For compost in the Calgary area, see the resources for Chapter 7 below.

• For questions to ask potential yard care providers regarding their eco-friendliness, put out by the Competition Bureau of Canada, see competitionbureau.gc.ca/epic/site/cb-bc.nsf/en/01154e.html.

• If you witness a yard care company in Canada that claims to be "green" but uses synthetic pesticides or makes other claims you consider misleading, complain to the Competition Bureau of Canada at 1-800-348-5358 or visit their website at competitionbureau.gc.ca.

In the U.S.A., contact the Federal Trade Commission Consumer Response Center at 1-866-382-4357 or ftc.gov under "Consumer Protection" and then "Environment."

• Search "pesticide-free yard sign" online to find one for your yard!
In Calgary, the Clean Calgary Association EcoStore has them. Call
403-230-1443, extension 222.

CHAPTER 5 – WEEDS AND BUGS

In this chapter, I relied heavily on the first two books below:

• *Weeds and Why They Grow* by Jay McCaman.
• *The Prairie Gardener's Book of Bugs: A Guide to Living with Common Garden Insects* by Nora Bryan and Ruth Staal.
• *Garden Bugs of Alberta: Gardening to Attract, Repel and Control* by Ken Fry, Doug Macaulay and Don Williamson is another good reference book.
• You should be able to find a book or resource on garden bugs for your region.

CHAPTER 6 – WHAT'S IN A LAWN?

• For compost and composted soil in the Calgary area, see the resources for Chapter 7 below.
• Grass seed—sheep's fescue alone and a low-maintenance mix—is available in homeowner-sized quantities from Bow Point Nursery, Springbank, Alberta. bowpointnursery.com.
Tel: 403-686-4434.
• For larger quantities of grass seed, search online or in the phone book under Seeds or Grass Seed Suppliers. Brett-Young and Northstar Seeds are good Canadian suppliers.
• *The Organic Lawn Care Manual* by Paul Tukey is a thorough reference book.

CHAPTER 7 – MAKING BEDS TO REPLACE YOUR LAWN

• Compost (for all around use), composted soil and arborist-cut wood chip mulch are available at Bow Point Nursery near Calgary in Springbank, Alberta. bowpointnursery.com.
Tel: 403-686-4434.
• Compost good for lawns (manure-based) and wood chips, for delivery in the Calgary area, are available from Western Canada Compost, westerncanadacompost.com. Tel: 403-251-9639.

- Compost good for perennial, tree and shrub beds (wood-based) and sawmill-composted wood chips, for delivery and pick-up in the Calgary area, are available from Top Spray in Cochrane. topspray.com. Tel: 403-932-1464.
- The Lasagna Gardening series of books by Patricia Lanza are fun and inspiring. Note that I differ from Lanza in a few respects. I advise using a thicker layer of newspaper than Lanza advises—use at least half a newspaper thick to prevent grass from coming through. Lanza is a fan of peat moss. I would rather natural peat bogs stay where they are in the wild.

CHAPTER 8 – SOIL: A FEEDING FRENZY

- *Teaming With Microbes: A Gardener's Guide to the Soil Food Web* by Jeff Lowenfels and Wayne Lewis of Alaska is the most accessible soil biology book.
- Elaine Ingham has many books on soil biology. The simple book is *Adding Biology*. Other books are her *Compost Tea Brewing Manual* and her *Field Guides 1 and 2* (compilations of emails she's sent over the years). She also has audio CDs on many topics related to soil biology.
- The books and CDs listed above, as well as some of the organic soil amendments recommended, are available from Sustainable Soil Solutions in Vulcan, Alberta, Canada. ssscinc.com. Tel: 403-485-6981.
- The international network of Soil Foodweb labs can provide soil biology testing for you, and most labs have advisors who can support you in improving the health of your yard for a fee. They should also have the above-mentioned books and CDs and other supplies. Check: soilfoodweb. com for the nearest lab to you. The Canadian Soil Foodweb labs are in Vulcan, Alberta: soilfoodweb.ca, and Halifax, Nova Scotia. Jolly Farmer in New Brunswick: jollyfarmer.com also does soil biology testing.
- The illustrations of the microbes at the root zone and in the soil are available for a licensing fee from the author. See her contact information at the end of this section.

CHAPTER 9 – THE WONDERS OF COMPOST

Classic books on composting

- *The Rodale Book of Composting*, Rodale Press.
- *Worms Eat My Garbage* by Mary Appelhof.

Resources on actively aerated compost tea

- eco-yards.com (my web site).
- soilfoodweb.com (the international network of Soil Foodweb labs).
- soilfoodweb.ca (the Canadian Soil Foodweb lab at Vulcan, Alberta).
- ssscinc.com (the sales company associated with the Vulcan lab—for supplies).
- intlctc.org (International Compost Tea Council).
- Search online for "compost tea bucket brewer" and you will find instructions for making your own.
- See the resources for Chapter 8 above for good books and other resources.

CHAPTER 10 – DESIGNING YOUR ECO-YARD

General design books

- *Front Yard Gardens: Growing More Than Grass* by Liz Primeau has photos of beautiful front yards across Canada. It's a great ideas book, and I show it to almost all my clients to get a sense of what they like.
- *Backyard Blueprints: Design, Furniture and Plants for a Small Garden* by David Stevens is also full of photos and ideas, and I use it to show clients when we are doing an enclosed yard.
- *Designing Alberta Gardens* by Jan Mather is a comprehensive guide to designing all kinds of gardens (e.g., woodland, color) and is applicable beyond Alberta.

Specialty design books

- *NatureScape Alberta: Creating and Caring for Wildlife Habitat at Home* by Myrna Pearman and Ted Pike is a comprehensive guide to making your yard a wildlife habitat. It includes topics such as plant selection and how to build bat houses and applies beyond Alberta.
- *The Tallgrass Restoration Handbook: for Prairies, Savannas and Woodlands*, edited by Stephen Packard and Cornelia F. Mutel. Applicable for tall grass prairie areas across North America.

Feng shui

- *Feng Shui in the Garden: Simple Solutions for Creating a Comforting, Life-affirming Garden of the Soul* by Nancilee Wydra.

Permaculture

- *Gaia's Garden: A Guide to Home-scale Permaculture* by Toby Hemenway.
- *Introduction to Permaculture* by Bill Mollinson.
- *Permaculture: A Designer's Manual* by Bill Mollinson (if you are serious, this is the full reference book).

Guidelines for choosing plants

Prairies/Northern Great Plains of North America
- Lois Hole's book series—*Perennial Favorites, Favorite Trees and Shrubs,* etc.—are really helpful. Besides photos and descriptions, the perennial book has lists of plants suited to different conditions, lists by plant color and a chart of when each blooms during the season.
- *Canada's Finest Hardy Plant Guide* by Bylands Nurseries Ltd. is a great resource for hardy trees and shrubs, including fruit trees, with photos and descriptions. The evergreens section is especially helpful. This book is available at garden centers and nurseries.
- *Native Plants for Prairie Gardens* by June Flanagan.
- *Perennials for the Prairies* by Sara Williams.
- *Best Groundcovers and Vines for the Prairies* by Sara Williams and Hugh Skinner.
- *Trees and Shrubs of Alberta* by Kathleen Wilkinson.
- The Wild About Flowers, ALCLA and Bedrock websites listed under "Suppliers – Alberta" below are all loaded with information about native wildflowers.

Eastern and Central North America
- *A Field Guide to Wildflowers—Northeastern and North Central North America* (Peterson Field Guides) by Roger Tory Peterson and Margaret McKenny is recommended by Caron Wenzel, who lives in the Chicago area and contributed to this book.
- *100 Easy-to-Grow Native Plants for Canadian Gardens* by Lorraine Johnson.

Shade plants
- *Favorite Shade Plants* by Marjorie Harris is written for all of Canada and the Northern United States.

Low-allergy plants
• *Allergy-free Gardening: The Revolutionary Guide to Healthy Landscaping* by Thomas Ogren has information on the allergy-affecting potential of many plants and lists of low-allergy plants.

Suppliers – Alberta
• Bow Point Nursery in Springbank, near Calgary, has native trees and bushes. bowpointnursery.com. Tel: 403-686-4434.
• ALCLA Native Plant Restoration in Brentwood, Calgary, has native wildflowers and some bushes. alclanativeplants.com. Tel: 403-282-6516.
• Wild About Flowers in Turner Valley has native wildflowers. wildaboutflowers.ca. Tel: 403-933-3903.
• Bedrock Seed Bank in Edmonton has native plants and seeds. bedrockseedbank.com. Tel: 780-785-7366.

Suppliers – North America
• Blazing Star Nursery in the Chicago area has native plants, seeds, houseplant and other plant care products as well as agricultural products. blazing-star.com. Tel: 815-338-4716.
• Many garden centers and nurseries are now selling native and hardy plants. Encourage them to bring in more!

CHAPTER 11 – WATER-WISE DESIGN

• *Designing the Prairie Xeriscape* by Sara Williams.
• *Landscape Guide for Canadian Homes* by Daniel Lefebvre and Susan Fisher for Canada Mortgage and Housing Corporation. This is a great general design, construction and landscaping book.

CHAPTER 12 – GROWING VEGETABLES

• For permaculture resources, see resources for Chapter 10 above and for lasagna gardening see Chapter 7 resources above.
• *All New Square Foot Gardening: Grow More in Less Space* by Mel Bartholomew.
• *How to Grow More Vegetables (and Fruits, Nuts, Berries, Grains, and Other Crops) Than You Ever Thought Possible on Less Land Than You Can Imagine* by John Jeavons features the double-dig bio-intensive method.

• *Brother Crow, Sister Corn: Traditional American Indian Gardening* by Carol Buchanan features the three sisters gardening method.

HIRE THE AUTHORS!

Caron Wenzel has contributed to the outline and philosophy of *Eco-yards* and also has written two chapters. She is available to do restoration consulting, talks and education. She is in the Chicago area. She also has a great shopping website with native plants and other products to support your eco-yard.

Caron Wenzel
Blazing Star Nursery
blazing-star.com
Tel: 815-338-4716

My company *eco-yards*™ is available to design an eco-yard for you and install it in Calgary, Alberta, whether it is a new yard or an existing yard. We also have an *eco-yards spray* service in Calgary, spraying actively aerated compost tea to keep your yard healthy. We sometimes do custom spray programs. Check out my website for more on my company's services.

I love talking about eco-yards, so hire me to do a talk or education program! For this, I would consider travelling.

If you want to order books, go to my website. To keep up with my latest *eco-yards*™ offerings, visit my website.

Laureen Rama
eco-yards™
eco-yards.com
Tel: 403-969-1176

Index

About the author

LAUREEN RAMA'S lifelong passion is beautifying landscapes in ways that enhance the natural environment. She has been landscaping most of her life, from helping her parents landscape yards as a child, in towns across Western Canada, to beautifying landscapes as an adult, inspired by travelling and living in different landscapes around the world and North America. Since 2008, Laureen has been running her own landscape design, installation and health business.

Laureen has a rich background, having worked as an international development educator, public involvement consultant, management consultant specializing in creativity, and shamanic healer and teacher.

Laureen has landscaping experience in Calgary and Edmonton, Alberta, on the Northern Great Plains east of the Rocky Mountains. *Eco-yards* has been written to apply almost anywhere.

If you have enjoyed *Eco-yards*, you might also enjoy other

BOOKS TO BUILD A NEW SOCIETY

Our books provide positive solutions for people who
want to make a difference. We specialize in:

**Sustainable Living • Green Building • Peak Oil
Renewable Energy • Environment & Economy
Natural Building & Appropriate Technology
Progressive Leadership • Resistance and Community
Educational & Parenting Resources**

New Society Publishers

ENVIRONMENTAL BENEFITS STATEMENT

New Society Publishers has chosen to produce this book on recycled paper made
with **100% post consumer waste**, processed chlorine free, and old growth free.
For every 5,000 books printed, New Society saves the following resources:[1]

26	Trees
2,335	Pounds of Solid Waste
2,570	Gallons of Water
3,352	Kilowatt Hours of Electricity
4,245	Pounds of Greenhouse Gases
18	Pounds of HAPs, VOCs, and AOX Combined
6	Cubic Yards of Landfill Space

[1]Environmental benefits are calculated based on research done by the Environmental Defense Fund
and other members of the Paper Task Force who study the environmental impacts of the paper
industry.

For a full list of NSP's titles, please call 1-800-567-6772 *or check out our website* at:

www.newsociety.com

NEW SOCIETY PUBLISHERS
Deep Green for over 30 years